PRAISE FOR THE L⁄

"Hard-hitting, explosive, and masterfully told. Whether battling drug traffickers on the streets of America, or hunting terrorists in the markets of Kabul, Tim Sellers is the stuff that legends are made of. He is a real life Captain America who is also the most sincere, big-hearted and compassionate person I've ever known. His book is both humorous and honest as it looks back at life on the streets—from the cringe worthy but hilarious moments that all of us have but few admit to, to the heroic highs of a life lived with unflinching courage!"

- *Steven "Batman" Peterson, DEA (retired); VP, National Law Enforcement Speakers Bureau, LLC*

"A truly humble, un-glittered, sometimes taut and yet sometimes hilarious accounting of the law enforcement career of one of the DEA's most highly-decorated American heroes, *The Last Cowboy* is also a boots-on-the-ground cross section of recent history, chronicling over 30 years of major threats to our country and criminal trends affecting directly and indirectly the lives of the American public. For a man who has spent most of his life vanquishing some of humankind's most dodgy individuals, Tim Sellers has, by some miracle, emerged not only alive and well, but with his humanity and humor firmly intact. That fact jumps off the page with every phrase depicting each real-life event we are privy to and privileged to get a glimpse of."

- *D. V. Caitlyn, Writer, Director, and Author of the screenplay, "Duty," which is based on the events in this book*

"Insurmountable odds, understated courage. Tim Sellers is a cop's cop with a warrior's edge. This man knows how to tell a story – utterly gripping page-turner. "

- *Lt. David Lundgren, Hayward Police Department; Medal of Valor recipient; President, California Narcotic Officers Association; California Narcotic Officer of the Year (2007)*

"Tim's international law enforcement opportunities have provided him with true-life experiences and an extraordinary insight in the drug underworld as it coexists with international and domestic terrorism. Tim continues to share his experiences and knowledge so that law enforcement officers can remain safe and alert."

- *Sam Candelaria, Detective, Albuquerque Police Department (retired); DEA Task Force Officer; NM Narcotics Officers Association; Police Writers Association*

"This man's story will forever change your ideas on what an American hero is. The battles for our freedom from fear are fought on the streets of America, our borders, and in faraway places. This is a powerful story written by a true American hero."

- *Paul Stevens, Special Agent, Minnesota Bureau of Criminal Apprehension (retired); President, National Drug Enforcement Officers Association*

"*The Last Cowboy* is a ripping account of one man's battle against terrorists and drug dealers along the Mexico border and Afghanistan. Sellers' work is a must-read for any patriotic American who understands the undeniable truth that society will descend into anarchy unless cowboys like Sellers are given open range. It is a potent work that the readers won't soon forget."

- *Peter F. Boyce, General Counsel, National Narcotics Officers Association, Inc*

"I tried to reason with him: 'Are you crazy?! Afghanistan is a war zone! You're too old and too close to retirement!' Tim, in his usual cowboy way, ignored my advice and went anyway. In this often hilarious and thoroughly stirring account, Tim's life in law enforcement is a call to others to live a courageous, authentic life that does what is right in spite of the opposition."

- *Gilbert Gonzalez, DEA (retired); Executive Director, Texas Narcotic Officers Association; DEA Award of Valor recipient*

"It is men like Tim Sellers who make the bad guys (in either war or peace), look back over their shoulder and walk a little bit faster."

- *E. Ramirez, LTC (retired), 10th Mountain Division veteran, OEF 2004*

THE LAST COWBOY

THE LAST COWBOY

THE TRUE STORY OF ONE OF DEA'S
MOST DECORATED UNDERCOVER AGENTS

TIM SELLERS

Charleston, South Carolina

THE LAST COWBOY

THE TRUE STORY OF ONE OF DEA'S
MOST DECORATED UNDERCOVER AGENTS

Published by Four Winds Books
PO Box 21597
Charleston, SC 29413
www.FourWindsBooks.org

The names and identifying details of some
characters in this book have been changed.

For information about discounts for bulk purchases,
please contact Four Winds Books Special Sales:
(843) 323-6822 or sales@fourwindsbooks.org

To schedule a speaking event, Tim can be contacted at:
www.TheLastCowboy.com or
www.BattleTerror.com

ISBN 978-0-9854127-0-8

Printed in the United States of America
First Edition 2012

I dedicate this book to my grandchildren

who were my inspiration for this endeavor

CONTENTS

ACKNOWLEDGEMENTS

I would like to thank my wife for the decades of unwavering love and support she has given me while I lived out my youthful dreams of riding the badlands with John Wayne, thumping black-hatted Bad Barts, or today's equivalent, the sleazy drug traffickers and terror dudes that make the good citizens silent. I don't think the government gives out rewards for that sort of thing, but they ought to. Without these young ladies, we would all be drunk, penniless, tattooed, bald with pony tails, hairy no-necks dripping with gold chains, unchurched, indicted, incarcerated, paroled, or just plain dead. Rather, I am just plain bald and attend church (though I drive real slow getting there). Not bad.

I would also like to thank my English professor daughter #1, who listened to me endlessly bend her ears and bounce off epiphanies into the wee hours of the morning while she juggled four kids, two dogs, her students, and one rather understanding husband. As you will soon learn, I have great difficulty coloring within the lines. But in forging this manuscript with the box of Crayola Crayons I borrowed from my grandchildren, I tried desperately to keep a steady hand. My daughter painstakingly corrected and enhanced my crude attempt to write my memoir, and for that I forever will be grateful. It was she who first trumpeted "publish" upon reading my chicken scratch. Her constant attention, insightful critique, and skillful editing helped to smooth out the rough edges and made hard work fun.

I want to thank my grandchildren for sharing their crayons with me. *The Last Cowboy* is an account of the life and times of their Daddy Pop, who wants them to grow up nourished by warm cookies and their Grammy's love, free from the cares of the troubled world that surrounds them.

I would like to thank my second daughter and my only son, for their encouragement and prayers: my youngest daughter, for her steadfast love, joyous praise, encouragement, and incredible belief in me regardless of the obvious, and my son, for his inspiring service to our country as a true warrior, gallant son, and best friend. He has assumed the point man position in our life patrol. My children and my wife were the protagonist quad who pressed me to publish this manuscript. The greatest gift a mother and father can enjoy is the love their children offer in return for the sleepless nights they endure in the course of raising them. Our children have given back more than we gave.

I will always be grateful to Matthew Pridgen of Four Wind Books who took a chance on an old cowboy from Texas and patiently brought us to the end of the trail. He is a mannered Southern visionary.

PROLOGUE

*We sleep safe in our beds because rough men stand ready in
the night to visit violence on those who would do us harm.*

George Orwell

Shaheed was a man intent on a deadly mission. We had tracked him
for over an hour and hoped to get close enough to foil his suicide
attack. Ahead of him were a couple of buses loading up passengers,
and he was determined to get himself a seat. His eyes locked on the
closest bus and the line of people that waited to get on board. He
pressed through the crowds towards the bus and attached himself to
the last man in line.

It was a nightmare. Once he got on that bus, it would be
impossible for us to stop what he had started. Afghans would surely
die, and if Shaheed reached his target, Americans or coalition forces
were going to die as well. The bus was now a weapon of war.

We were involved in a joint operation, with Jeff Higgins and me
the lone representatives from the Drug Enforcement Administration.
Norwegian Special Forces, in cooperation with the US military,
rounded out our group. As DEA agents, we knew that our mode of
operation differed from the others in our group. We weren't so
concerned with rules and regulations (so long as we got our guy),
and the others were trained to abide by them strictly. We were

considered long-haired mavericks, and I'm sure our inclusion in the mission might have raised suspicions that things might get a little outside of their comfort zones. And that's where we played best—outside of other people's comfort zones. We were rough and ready to deal, trained by years of working with the same kind of scum we were trailing today.

Once, twice, three times we requested permission from command to apprehend Shaheed. Denied. It was still too dangerous, as the Norwegian Special Forces were trapped across the Kabul River. Afghans outnumbered us one hundred to one, and command didn't like those odds.

The deadly bomb, gripped tightly in Shaheed's hand, was wrapped in an innocent looking pepto-pink plastic bag. No one on the bus suspected Shaheed's mission. Not one of his potential victims knew his purpose. But we did, and we struggled for the green light from the higher-ups back at command to get out of that surveillance vehicle and do what so urgently needed to be done.

We were mere yards away from a man who carried a bomb commissioned for staggering carnage. Flesh and blood, when caught unaware, would be helpless against its destructive power. And yet, there we were, flesh and blood—ironically the only things that stood between it and its prey. We were painfully aware of its presence. How could we not act? It wasn't even a thought.

I told the Marine to ask for orders to arrest Shaheed once again as I saw Shaheed make his move into the bus. We moved now, or the unthinkable alternative happened. Before the Marine completed his request, I bolted from the car with Jeff close behind me. I couldn't wait for permission that we knew wasn't coming.

"Sir, it's too late. DEA's out of the car."

CHAPTER ONE

GREENHORN

WIRED UP

The coffee smelled as if it had been on the burner since the morning. With each step, I spilled a little on the floor. Victor Maldonado, my partner, followed me into the room illuminated by a buzzing fluorescent light. Maldonado sat down at the wobbly wooden desk across the room from Larry. I approached Larry and placed my hand on the back of his chair as Vic read him his Miranda warning. Vic and I were police officers together in El Paso, Texas in the mid-seventies, a time when police officers could do what we did to Larry without the fear of losing it all in a lawsuit. For a man like me who broke out into hives when rules got in the way of catching the crook, it was the best of times. Don't get me wrong—I appreciated the law. Heck, I *was* the law. But sometimes we had to get creative. Like we did with Larry.

Larry's eyes darted nervously around the room. He waived his rights and agreed to talk to us. I sensed his anxiety and offered him a cigarette to help calm him down. I walked over to the desk Vic sat at and dug in the drawers for some cigarettes. I found a half-empty package of Lucky Strikes and tossed them to Larry. Vic handed him some matches. Larry lit up.

We suspected that Larry had ripped off a store of some firearms. He was an employee at a sporting goods store and the only one in a position to do it, according to the manager. So we picked him up. It became apparent as we interviewed him that Larry was not the sharpest tool in the shed. We were determined to find out the truth as we began to grill him.

"C'mon, Larry. You either did it or know who did."

"Man, I didn't do it."

"Listen—we're going to find out who did it. We always do. Save yourself the trouble, Larry."

"I told you—I don't know nothin', and I didn't do nothin' either!"

The more we questioned Larry, the more we became concerned that he was not our man. We suspected that he knew something about the theft, but was not necessarily involved, as he had difficulty explaining a lot of his actions and continued to proclaim his innocence. We changed course and started to probe Larry about his associates. Larry started to get anxious and began to rub his knees with his open hands.

The tension had mounted sufficiently enough to press him about whom he suspected of stealing the firearms. He wouldn't give it up.

I began to pace back and forth between Larry's chair and the door. Larry gripped the side arms of his chair as we ran out of ways to ask him the same questions, over and over. We were both disappointed in Larry's answers, and we had to pull a rabbit out of our hat or let him go.

Much to my relief, a vapor of an idea wriggled its way into my thoughts, and my imagination began to give it shape and substance. I decided to take a chance.

"Would you be willing to take a polygraph examination?"

Larry slid to the back of his chair and stared toward the floor, as if to carefully consider whether his acquiescence in the matter would help or hurt his case. After a moment or two, he meekly replied, "Sure, I guess."

I looked at Vic and said that I would return in a few moments after warming up the polygraph machine. At that moment, Vic looked up at me with that deer-in-the-headlights look. He knew that we didn't have a polygraph machine, let alone the training to conduct polygraph examinations. Ignoring Vic's questioning look, I walked out and went to the supply room to scrounge around for any kind of electronics we could hook Larry up to.

In my absence, Larry struggled to calm himself and asked Vic how long the examination would last. Vic ignored him and continued to press him for the truth. I had fully expected Larry to succumb to the pressure before I returned to the interrogation room. He didn't. Because I found myself in quite a precarious situation, I had to make do.

I asked Larry to follow me into an adjoining copy room, and Larry obediently followed me, with Vic in tow. When we entered the room, I asked Larry to be seated in a chair, which was flush against a large copying machine.

I reached down and wrapped a leather belt around Larry's ankle and strapped him to the leg of the chair. Grinning ear to ear, I stood up at Larry's side and snuck a look at Vic. Vic suddenly realized what was happening and began to laugh uncontrollably. He quickly left the office and closed the door behind him to hide his laughter. I had to do everything I could to keep from laughing right along with Vic. After regaining his composure, Vic walked back in.

I placed a wire in each of Larry's hands. After taping one to Larry's left wrist, I instructed him to hold his wrist tightly to the side of the chair. I taped a second wire to the tip of Larry's right thumb and asked him to hold it six inches from his ear. The wires led to an old radio transmitter in which the back was removed, and this exposed a number of tubes, switches, and multicolored wires. I placed the transmitter on top to the copying machine and secured it with tape.

I warned Larry to be perfectly still, as any movement might affect the accuracy of the examination. Taking a deep breath, Larry nodded in acknowledgement. I asked him to relax, breath normally, and keep quiet because the test was about to begin. We began the examination by asking him his name.

He replied, "Larry."

"Your whole name, please," I asked.

"Larry Roland Smith," he said, clearing his throat nervously.

"Where do you live?"

"Over in Channel View…say, you know where I live!" he exclaimed.

Vic retorted with, "Yeah, Larry, but the machine doesn't."

"Oh yeah," he murmured.

The questions continued for half an hour. Vic began to increase the intensity of the examination and machine-gunned the questions. Larry moved about nervously in anticipation of each question. When he answered his questions, I pushed the copy button, causing the machine to sputter, crunch, whorl, and crank out a sheet of paper. Following a barrage of questions meant to build up his anxiety, Vic finally asked him who stole the firearms. I simultaneously hit the copy machine four or five times, which caused it to go berserk, spewing sheets of paper everywhere.

Larry leapt from his chair, tore the wires from his hands, and fell flat on his face as he had neglected to unfasten the leather strap securing his leg. Larry couldn't contain it any longer, and he began to scream curse words at the top of his lungs.

"It was Ray! Ray did it—he stole those guns! I had nothin' to do with it! Ray bragged about how he pulled it off. I don't want to get involved, man!" Larry collapsed on the floor in a twisted pretzel. I grabbed Larry's arms and dragged him to his feet.

He could have saved us a lot of trouble if he had just given it up in the beginning. But he didn't, which gave us no choice but to break out the big gun (or so to speak, the copy machine).

It was the start of an unconventional career in law enforcement, made so by my rejection of cookie-cutter recommendations for keeping the snakes in the snake pit. I figured it was my job to throw as many snakes into the pit as I could, and I was determined to do just that, even if it meant that I didn't stick closely to the regulations. I knew that the powers that be couldn't complain too much if I accomplished the mission, no matter how creative I had to be to get it done.

It all began with my transformative years in the El Paso Police Department in which I honed my freestyle police tactics that earned me the reputation of a cowboy. In my mind, I couldn't think of a better compliment. To a few supervisors, I was an unpredictable renegade who made an early retirement for themselves look mighty attractive. I preferred to think of myself as the guy in the white hat— a cowboy who operated in a wild frontier filled with deadbeats and dealers...a man who tried to keep the bad in check so the good could flourish. But the journey from tenderfoot to seasoned undercover agent was not smooth at all, my friend. Not smooth at all.

RICHARD THE LIONHEARTED

I didn't start out bending the rules. I began my career in law enforcement as a police officer in the city of El Paso, Texas in 1974. My first training partner, Richard Perez, was a crusty old fart. I had recently graduated from the El Paso Police Academy and was partnered up with him to teach me the ropes. I was a youngster and still very polite and unschooled in the ways of the big, bad world. "Sir…yes, sir…no, sir!" My politeness irritated Richard to no end. Richard was everything your mother warned you about, but was also one of the smartest, street-wise guys I had ever met. I was a rookie in every sense of the word.

Initially, we did not hit it off. I was like an anchor. Poor Richard grew very frustrated with the way I drove, the way I spoke Spanish, my politeness…heck, just about everything about me. It seemed like he criticized everything I did. When I stood up to him, he just stopped talking to me. It was real hard riding around all night with a mannequin in a blue suit.

Every time we picked up a prisoner he would make me ride in the back with them. It started to get real old. One day we got a call to pick up a shoplifter at a local department store. When we arrived, Richard told me to wait outside with the motor running while he went in to pick up the shoplifter. I was a little tired of this drill. I knew what came next: he was going to tell me to get in the back seat with the crook, and I was expected to dutifully obey.

Not this time. I was going to exercise my rights as a seasoned two-month patrolman. I slid over to the driver's seat and locked the front doors. When Richard walked out, he found me sitting in his seat and told me to get out. No way—I wasn't going to move. I flashed a big Cheshire cat grin in his direction and tightened my grip around the steering wheel. At this point, he got real mad and I am talking *real* mad. Not your run-of-the-mill "I'm ticked" mad, but "I'm-gonna-break-your-neck-if-you-don't-get-out-of-my-seat-rookie" mad. I didn't budge. And neither did he. He walked back inside and called another unit to pick him and the prisoner up so they didn't have to ride in our patrol car. When the other police car arrived, he climbed inside with the prisoner, and they drove him all the way to the police station. I followed like a whipped dog in our car. When I arrived, he checked in the prisoner, walked out, climbed into the vacated driver's seat of our patrol car, and drove stone quiet the rest of the day.

When we ended the shift, he bailed from the patrol car like it was on fire and stomped away. Things just didn't seem to lighten up after this point. It was plain to see that he did not like a rookie who stood up to him or even a rookie in his presence at all. I cramped his style, but that's to be expected of a rookie.

ROAST PIG

My six-month probationary period began when I left the police academy. I finally got to put my training in action, and it was an exhilarating experience. I don't think my training partner, Richard, felt exactly the same way. It may have had something to do with the fact that I was not very bright, or just a baby cop in need of direction. Regardless, he paid a dear price for turning me loose from time to time. In this case, it was a heart-stopping moment, at least for my partner Richard.

On the night in question, we cruised around the old 53 District that was right outside Ft. Bliss, a large Army base, and runs through the Five Points neighborhood in central El Paso to the border with Mexico. The Five Points neighborhood is the heart of Old El Paso, a mix of older brick and stucco residences and small family businesses at the base of the Franklin Mountains. From the many porches that grace the old traditional homes, one can see the streets of Juarez, Mexico. At night, the low voltage lights of this enormous Mexican city glimmer lightly in the distance. Five Points and old Northeast begins at the conclusion of Pershing Drive, where the name changes to Dyer Street. The lower part of Dyer Street in the 1970s was loaded with low-rent apartments, bars, street thugs, and hookers. Our call number was 253, the two denoting that we worked out of Central Division and the 53 being our District. It was late in the afternoon, and the sun began to beat down hard on us that hot, summer day.

As we drove down one of the side streets that ran off Dyer, we noticed a large group of men crowded around a bonfire. We saw them throw pieces of furniture, scrap wood, trash, and anything else they could find into the fire to stoke it. The fire burned in between two one-story apartment buildings and rose to heights above the rooflines.

They turned and looked at us, watching as we slowed down to a stop and parked alongside the curb. They started to get a little agitated as they waited for our reaction and we could tell that they expected the worst. I looked over at my partner and waited for some direction.

Ol' Richard didn't even look at me and said, "Go tell them to put the fire out. I'll wait."

I looked at him dumbfounded and replied, "Huh?"

Richard snapped back, "I'll wait in the patrol car, call for help if they jump you, and then bail from the car to pull you from the flames." Now that was encouraging. There were no portable radios in those days that enabled us to call for help when we were in the thick of it. Speaking of flames, I might have gotten help a little faster if we had used smoke signals.

As I stepped out of the patrol car, I thought about it a second and figured Richard was probably right (like I knew?). I hoped I might lighten things up a bit and give Richard a run for his money. I looked over at the group of men, now staring intently at me, and began to strut slowly towards them in a swagger John Wayne would have loved.

I probably swung my hips a little too much, but everyone got the message that I meant business. Richard told me later that when he saw me walk over there, he thought I was a dead man walking and reached for the radio just in case.

There must have been nearly fifty of them. Heck, maybe it was closer to two hundred. Well, there were at least thirty anyway. They all stared at me in disbelief that I would dare step on their turf and waited for me to get close enough to throw me in the flames. And flames there were—the closer I got, the hotter it got.

As I walked toward the crowd, I looked for the biggest man there. I knew if I took him down first, the crowd would back down and succumb to my commanding presence. In the back of the crowd, closest to the flames, stood the largest man I had ever seen. He was so tall that his head seemed to rise three feet above everyone else's. I headed straight for him, focused and ready to launch a frontal assault on that bad boy.

As I approached the crowd, they parted in the middle as I pushed forward. I felt like Moses parting the Red Sea. Stepping through the crowd, they enclosed behind me and completely cut me off from escape. Escape? Never. I intended to end this matter. My way. Mano a mano.

I could hear the elevated breathing of my captors as they mumbled unspeakable things. Chains unraveled, guns were cocked, and there was plenty of cursing. I pressed on, certain that if I failed it would be the end of me.

I looked forward unwaveringly, focused on this mountain of a man, and stepped boldly towards him. The closer I got, the darker the sky became, as he stood between the fire and me. He rose so high before me that he blotted out the fire and the surrounding light from the sun. It was like a total eclipse.

My brow began to sweat from the intense heat of the fire. I squared off before him, but he was unmoved as I leaned into him and stared into his belly button. I lifted my eyes and forced him to meet my hardened gaze. It was as if time stopped. There was not a noise to be heard. Everyone in the crowd leaned with me to hear what I had to say as well as learn their motive for pulverizing me. I hesitated a moment to increase the dramatic tension and said in my most confident-sounding voice, "Hey, you got any marshmallows?"

That did it. Everyone cracked up with laughter. There was backslapping and hee-hawing all over the place. The big man bellowed out loud that I was one fine officer and reached out his tree trunk of an arm to grab my hand and shake it. As I walked away, I looked back and told all those knuckleheads to put the fire out and go home. Richard was sure I was a dead man but I guess he was wrong. A little humor goes a long way.

URINAL STANDOFF

We worked graveyards near the intersection of Dyer Street and Fred Wilson Boulevard. There used to be a gas station on the corner in the olden days. The station owner would keep the outside restroom open for us all night long, even though he closed up shop in the late evening.

Whenever we had to take a break, we would drive up and take care of business, one at a time. We rolled up one early morning hour, and I went inside while Richard stayed outside in the patrol car while the engine ran to listen to the radio for calls.

I walked inside and closed the door. I stood in front of the urinal and began to unsnap the leather strap that held my revolver down. I was pretty proud of myself, looking all spiffy in that crisp, new uniform. Snap. Unsnap. Snap…unsnap…snap…unsnap…uh, oh. While messing with my revolver I accidently, without thinking, pulled back the hammer, and it locked. I don't know how someone does that without intending, to but I succeeded in doing it. I was new at this gig.

My mind began to race: "Oh boy. Now what was it that they taught me at the academy? Let's see…carefully remove your revolver and point it in a safe direction." In my case, that was towards the urinal. "Place your thumb between the hammer and the frame and slowly disengage the hammer while you pull the trigger…ever so carefully…easy…easy…"

"BANG!!!"

The urinal crashed down on the floor. The deafening sound reverberated off the tiled walls. This did not bode well for a career in law enforcement. I realized in a fraction of a second that if Richard ever got wind of this I would never hear the end of it. Ever. I had to think fast…really fast.

I holstered the weapon just as Richard crashed through the door. I saw his mouth moving but couldn't hear a thing, just the ringing in my ears. I was stone deaf. It looked like he asked what had happened. I just pointed to the urinal and exclaimed that it just fell to the floor! He sighed and signaled with his head to follow him.

When we got into the police car, I knew that a call came in because Richard picked up the mic to speak into it. Richard turned to me and started to talk ninety miles an hour, none of it heard by me. Richard then pulled the red light lever and left skid marks a mile long as we dashed out of the parking lot headed down Dyer Street.

His face looked tight with suspense, and I sat there wondering where the heck we were going. I had to pretend that I'd heard everything that he had said, while I prepared myself to be ready for whatever I was going to have to do. I didn't know how long I was going to be able to keep it up, but I was going to do whatever it took to keep Richard from finding out what a Barney Fife I was. Little did

I know that this evening began my slow transformation into a tried and true street cop.

TURN OUT THE LIGHTS

We headed south through Five Points and towards the 51 District. The 51 District was a tough nut. The main drag, Alameda Street, bisected the entire length of 51 and was lined with bars, warehouses, and small shops. The closer we got to Alameda, the more I started to hear. It was a good thing, as I soon learned we were headed to the old Mine and Mill Bar on Alameda Street. A large union party was being held there and had gotten out of hand. The police unit assigned to the area, 251, had already warned them that if they had to return, they would shut it down.

Apparently, the police dispatch continued to receive calls on the party boys and sent 251 back. This time, the cops called for backup. With hundreds of boozed-up revelers inside, the unit that called for backup expected the worst.

When we rolled up, there were already three other two-man units there, parlaying outside. We ran up just as they made their way up to the door. Joe Segovia, the senior officer in 251, quickly told us while we walked to the door that when he was here last, there was one loud-mouthed meatball who screamed out "pig" and other choice words to try to incite the crowd to throw the cops out.

Joe told us that he would go inside and flip the light switch to signal the end of the party and then order everyone out. Joe wanted someone to single out that meatball and arrest him when they funneled everyone out the door. With only eight cops and two to three hundred union men, this was a tall order—but we weren't going home without someone in bracelets.

Joe walked in and flipped the switch. Five of the cops lined up outside and formed a line that extended out from the door while Richard and I stood to the side behind the cops and the crowd as it passed through the door. The crowd was not happy, but complied. Richard and I looked inside and waited for Joe to point out the pot-stirrer. Joe studied the crowd and pointed out a guy who was trying to hide in their midst as they came forward towards the door. He was bobbing up and down in the back and tried to stay in the middle, hidden from Joe's watchful eyes.

As the crowd stepped outside, they came together in a group to form their opposition to us. The dirtball instigator finally surfaced. He was so massive that he filled the doorframe as he passed through, hanging his head to hide from Joe. He was a large, obese man, who had biceps the size of fifty-pound sacks of potatoes. I was not sure we could even get him through the row of cops who separated us without breaking the line and leave an opening wide enough to drive a truck through. Joe pointed him out to us again, and we made our move.

JOY RIDE

We reached between the cops, pulled the behemoth through, and thrust him up against the wall. We knew we only had a few moments to hook him up and throw him in the backseat of our patrol car before the crowd turned on us. Well, that was not to be done. With him slammed up against the wall, we attempted to pull his arms behind him and cuff his wrists. Richard could only get one cuff on when it became apparent that he was too large. It was not physically possible to press his arms together to the rear close enough to secure the second cuff.

We pressed hard as we heard the crowd start to scream at us to let him go. We had run out of time and decided to just drag him to the patrol car and throw him in the back seat. While we dragged him to the patrol car, the crowd started to push through the line of cops that separated us to take him back. I opened the back door, and Richard and I shoved him from behind as hard as we could and finally succeeded. He filled the entire rear cavity above the back seat. I squeezed in on top of him and tried to hold him down while Richard jumped in the driver's seat and sped away.

I looked out the rear window and saw all the cops loading up and getting out of Dodge. We heard Joe on the police radio shouting out that all of the union boys were coming to the central station to take our prisoner away and called for all the city police to come downtown to protect the station house.

Just to paint you a picture of my predicament, my biggest concern was not the union thugs taking our prisoner away, but keeping this big ox that I was perched on from rising up and slamming me against the ceiling of the patrol car.

I had my doubts that we would even make it to the station house. These were in the days of open patrol cars, with no hard plastic windows to separate the back from the front seats, which left the driver vulnerable to attack if the prisoner was not secured. Which he, of course, was not.

Sure enough, he must have read my mind. He rose up and pressed me against the ceiling and started to twist, turn, and buck. I was like a rag doll as he just tossed me off of him. He whipped up on me with his fists as he flailed his arms about on the inside of the vehicle, occasionally hammering Richard in the process. Richard was driving about 150 mph towards the stationhouse and seemed oblivious to the dirtball thrashing about. He was resolved to get us there.

In the meantime, I knew I was going to have to get this guy under control, or we were going to crash and burn. So I cut loose with a flurry of hits to the face and head. He just angrily glared at me while he continued his assault on anything that moved. I threw everything I had at him, to no avail. He kept swinging and cussing as we fought face-to-face in the back seat, exchanging punches. Problem was, I felt all of his, and he was like a sponge that just soaked up each hit and slammed mine back.

Suddenly, I saw his head jack around like a punching bag as it took hits from the front seat. I couldn't see what was hitting him, but whatever it was, it made contact and hit hard. I looked over at Richard and he still drove like a bat out of Hades, but his eyes were glued to the rear-view mirror as he directed his assault on this hamburger's head with multiple hits from his baton. He swung with the accuracy of a brain surgeon as he precisely measured each swing to center on this monster's head and just pass my head by a matter of millimeters. I was amazed.

Did this succeed in stopping the threat that this man posed against us? No. He shook it off and kept swinging. We had to get a handle on this guy or we were doomed. Richard drove like a coyote on fire until he suddenly slowed down and pushed the lever, turning off the red lights. Richard pulled over into an alleyway to hide from the union boys who might pass by while we dealt with this meatball. Richard stopped the patrol car and walked to the back door and opened it. The meatball and I poured onto the pavement in a twisting, turning mass of swinging arms and legs. Richard pulled me from him and I struggled to my feet. The meatball followed me upward and stood facing both of us in a challenge for us to bring it on.

It seemed like an eternity as we stared back at him, waiting for him to make his move. He did. He ducked his head downward and charged at us like a bull on a rampage. As he closed in on me, I unleashed my secret weapon, a tightly gripped nightstick hidden behind my forearm. I whipped it out and hit him in the head right after I stepped aside to allow him to pass me by. He continued on and crashed into the side of the patrol car, dropping to the ground with a resounding thud. Richard and I looked at each other in wonderment. I commented that felling the beast was easier than I thought it would be. We scraped him up off the pavement, and this time we cuffed him in front and poured him into the back seat. Richard threw the car into gear, and we were off.

ROUGH CROWD

We heard radio chatter all the way downtown. They had rounded up all the units in town and had positioned themselves inside the sally port on one side of the police department. The sally port had a steel security screen that raised and lowered over the side entrance to the police department and was designed to prevent anyone from entering the secured area where prisoners were offloaded. Patrol cars would drive under the raised security screen, down into the basement, offload their prisoners, and then drive to the other identically fortified exit on the other side.

The security screen had been lowered to prevent the outside crowd from entering. When we drove up, we were met by about seventy-five angry, screaming toads that stood outside of the sally port. They were unaware that we had not yet arrived with the prisoner as we drove through the crowd, as our prisoner was lying flat on the back seat. As we approached the security screen, it was raised and the cops moved outside to hold back the crowd as we drove under the police department. The cops followed us in, and they closed the security screen. The crowd threw bottles and rocks at the screen, demanding the release of the prisoner.

Richard parked the patrol car, and we pulled the prisoner from the back seat. He was still out cold when we planted him in the report room and asked the lieutenant to watch him as we ran back to the entrance. The cops and the dirtballs were at a standoff, with several of the crowd still tossing things at the security fence. Well, Rich and I were fed up with these lowlifes, and I told one of the cops to stand by the gate and raise it intermittently while we snatched a person or two from the crowd. They slowly raised the fence and Richard and I ran out and each snatched a dirtball and dragged them inside, down the slanted driveway, into the basement, and then on to the report room. We secured them with the lieutenant and returned bringing down two more, and this continued until we had arrested a total of fourteen dirtballs. This effectively ended the matter, except that we spent the rest of the night doing paper to justify our actions.

When we were done, we still had an hour left to patrol so we headed out. It was daylight, and we were bushed. I drove while Richard kind of faded and slipped back into his mannequin state again and that was that.

While he zoned out, I thought of the long night, which began with my sinking a toilet and finished with taking down Goliath. I was pretty pleased with myself. I learned later that Rich was pretty pleased with me as well.

We became close friends over the years, and I learned how to live long and prosper working the hard streets of central El Paso under his watchful eye. He was fearless. Oh, the stories I cannot share. We spent more time in internal affairs explaining our actions than we spent getting into more trouble, which was probably a good thing. Internal affairs couldn't get a grip on us. We were pigs, yes, but we were greased pigs.

When a citizen needed help...he called a policeman. When a cop needed help...he called Richard.

RUSSELL STREET MEET

I really liked working with Ed Lisowski. Ed was a military veteran and sported a shock of red hair that sprouted from his head in such a way that his head looked like it was on fire. The graveyard shifts passed quickly with Ed as we yakked all night during our patrols in the old 53 District. The thing I really appreciated about him was that I was obviously still a rookie, and he didn't bring it up. He treated me as an equal. I had about six months on the job and felt good. A little too good. Cops have a tendency to feel shielded by that badge they wear on their chest, and I was not an exception.

I spoke a command and people jumped. A movement of my arm shifted traffic in any direction I pointed. You get comfortable with the idea that you are respected and no one would cross the line. You are safe behind that small badge that is pinned on your chest. And then there was Russell Street.

We had been patrolling the neighborhoods off Dyer Street when we got a radio call. To date ourselves, I need only tell you what kind of call it was: "Pot Party in Progress." Now that sounds a little dated of course, but in those days it meant something. Pot was a big deal. People went to jail for a long time for possession of only an ounce. Pot was a relatively new phenomenon, given the rise in popularity in the 1960s, and this was 1974.

Ed wheeled the patrol car around, and we drove to the address on Russell Street. We rolled to a stop in the front yard. There were no curbs and no grass (except what they were smoking). Standing in the front yard were about twelve gangsters, just loitering about. They looked up, saw us, and began to run like cockroaches do when the lights come on. They hurried past the small adobe house that was on the same lot.

We casually got out of the patrol car and called them back.

Slowly, a few returned, followed by the rest. We intended to tell them to knock it off and then be on our way, but they were a little thickheaded. They gathered in front of the small house. I spoke first and told them that we were getting phone calls on them. Ed and I could smell the pot, but were not that interested in making a big deal about it, as there were bigger fish to fry.

They were a little ticked off, to say the least. We had interrupted their party and besides, no one had been arrested for at least a week, so they were looking for relief from boredom. The mouthing up-ticked to graphic.

The pecking order became clear as the biggest dude there, Roberto, broke from the back of the crowd and came at me. I grabbed his neck and pulled him to the ground to cuff him. I really knew this was going to spark a riot, but what choice did I have? Dog pile. They all came down on top of Roberto and me. I had succeeded in getting one cuff on this punk, but failed to get the other on before I found myself in a pork sandwich, surrounded by a dozen meatballs.

Ed started to yank all of the crooks off of me while he sprayed his mace in massive streams all over my attackers (and me, I might add). He finally freed me and pulled me up while I still held on to Roberto with both hands. We dragged Roberto over to the patrol car, which by now was demolished. The front windshield had been smashed out, and there were dents scattered all over the car. They were still in the process of tearing up our patrol car as I tried to muscle Roberto into the back seat and Ed reached for the radio to call for back up.

Roberto stiffened up outside of the back door of the patrol car, and I kneed him in the groin to double him up. Waves of gangsters still came at us with sticks and anything else they could find to dislodge Roberto from our grip. They finally succeeded before Ed and I could press Roberto into the backseat of our patrol car. They pulled him away and gathered up in front of us for a final assault. Roberto picked up an iron garden chair and ran towards me as he held it above his head in an attempt to crash it down on my head. I pulled out my gun and pointed it at Roberto's head and told him to make his move. Ed was busy fighting off several of these bozos when we both heard sirens in a distance and knew that the cavalry was coming.

Roberto's eyes were glazed over and filled with anger as he started to swing the chair at my head. At this very moment, a patrol car with its siren screaming and red lights flashing broke the corner and flew to our sides. Roberto and his cockroaches turned and ran. I beat a path behind Roberto as he turned to run to the house. He made the porch, opened the screen door, and ran inside with me in hot pursuit.

I crashed through the screen door and rushed inside within an arm's reach of Roberto. Problem was, I was within arm's reach of his mother as well, who joined in the procession, close to my heels in pursuit. She smacked me with a frying pan as we plowed a path through the hallway. I tackled Roberto as he broached the bedroom door, and we crashed along with his mother in a pile of twisted bodies, covered with dirty, stinky clothes and a wooden chest of drawers. A couple of cops pulled us apart and finished cuffing Roberto.

Ed had his hands full as well as he chased down two of the gangsters into the alleyway and knocked them down. He dragged them both into the welcoming arms of several patrolmen who had come to our rescue.

When it was over, we had arrested eight of these thugs. We split them up between the patrol cars, with Ed and me taking four of them. Ed drove, and I turned around in the front seat to watch our prisoners as Ed lit out for downtown. I looked over at Ed, and he sported a black eye, cut head, and a torn uniform. We both got hammered pretty good. I was cut up and sore from all the hits I took, but we were both glad to be alive. Our patrol car was a wreck, but it still drove. Ed looked over and asked me what happened to my badge. It was gone, ripped from my shirt. A good citizen who found it in his backyard turned it in a few days after the incident.

It was a week before Ed and I recuperated from our injuries, but mine ran a little deep. I learned that a badge is not a shield from harm and has no true ability to make a cop invincible, no matter how it makes him feel.

The other thing I took away from this was the strength and brotherhood that a cop shares with his partner. Ed and I did nothing that all cops don't do from time to time, but this was our shared experience of near death. It was ours as we stood toe to toe and kept each other alive. Ed's my hero.

DRUNK IN EL PASO

Sometimes I just can't help myself. I really try to obey the law. I work really hard at it (mostly). But life does not always work that way. It's not always black and white with clear, easy choices. I am not proud of my propensity to engage "Sellers Law," but sometimes circumstances demand it. I have to sleep at night knowing that I did the right thing, regardless of the consequences.

Family fights are the fodder for the patrolman's time sheets. The evening does not pass without at least one call to put out a fire at someone's home—a fire of passion, ignited by the inability to reason and followed by a flare-up that can only be extinguished by the blue suit.

One particular night was no different than any other. We got a

Signal 58—a "family fight" call—late one hot summer night in central El Paso. We moseyed over to the area and had a little difficulty finding the address. It was a small, old clapboard house tucked away in an alley hidden from the street. There was no streetlight to illuminate the area, and the darkness gave us a sense of foreboding. We rolled up and walked to the front door. The light was on inside. It lit up the kitchen, which was visible through the two-foot square window on the wooden door. Peering inside, we saw a woman who stood with her head hung downward in obvious distress. Her pants were partially pulled down, and she quietly cried.

We knocked on the door. She looked over at us and did not move. It was as if her feet were glued to the floor. She just continued to cry, but struggled against it. Her body would shake as she fought to hold still. We knocked a second time.

No response. Suddenly a tattooed male entered the room and yelled, "What do you want?" He glared at us and stood away from the door.

"Police, sir. We got a call. Is everything okay?"

"Get off my porch! No one called you. You got no right to be here!"

He looked at her and shouted, "Did you call them?" She shook her head from side to side. We asked him to open the door. "You got a warrant?" We, of course, did not. He taunted us, "I don't have to let you in!" I kicked in the door and pushed him out of the way, standing between him and the woman.

He started to yell at us. "You've got no right to be in my house. Get out! Now!" I asked the woman if she wanted to leave, and she just stood there. He screamed at her to keep her mouth shut. It was obvious that he frightened her.

We decided to probe a little further: "Has he hit you?" Still she stood there staring at the floor with her body shaking, half clothed.

He continued to scream that this was "his house" and told us to get out as he pointed to the door.

In Texas, a man's home is his castle. He was right. We had no right to be there. We did not see any physical assault. We could offer her safe haven but that was it. My partner separated them by dragging him to another room. I quietly asked her again if she wanted to leave with us. She only looked up and said she had nowhere to go.

The law protected him. My partner could not reason with him. He was furious. Irrational. On the edge of violence. We smelled alcohol on his breath as he edged his way back into the kitchen. We could not arrest him in his own home. It was clearly an evening that would end without justice. We had no alternative but to leave. Or did we?

I had about enough of this loud-mouthed bully. Just as he bellowed out his final demand for us to leave with his finger poking into my chest, I stopped him mid-sentence and grabbed him. I dragged him kicking and screaming through the kitchen to the back door and threw him down the stairs to the ground. Pouncing on him with a thud, I grabbed his arms and pulled them behind his back and cuffed him. He was right. We couldn't arrest him in his home for tormenting his wife or even drinking…but we could arrest him for public intoxication if we encountered him outside. Which we did.

I slept well knowing that this woman was safe at least for this one night. It was up to her to make the next move. I could only lead her to water, but it was up to her to drink from the well of life and never return to this scoundrel. I hope that she risked it and never returned, but this is something that I won't know this side of eternity.

CHAPTER TWO

BUSTIN' BRONCS

CAT AND RAT

I left the police department in late 1976 and moved to Houston, Texas with the Bureau of Alcohol, Tobacco, and Firearms as a Special Agent. This was the beginning of my career as a freestyle federal agent, which really was the norm in the late seventies. Law enforcement was a lot of fun without the many rules in place today that protect the agent from himself. It was the beginning of a wonderful life.

I remember meeting a female snitch (informant) back in '77. I never called my boss, and I didn't have to. I had met the snitch at an icehouse. This was not the kind of place that sells large chunks of ice, but a Houston-style beer joint. Anyone can run one. All you need is an abandoned house, an ice chest full of beer, and a few card tables. Build it, and they will come. This young lady called one day and said she wanted to work off her boyfriend's debt to society. He was in the Harris County jail, and she missed him enough to play the dangerous game of snitching someone off to the feds for a reduced sentence for her boyfriend. She was a meth head and ran with a rough crowd. One of her friends was a member of the Bandido Motorcycle Gang. This dude was supposed to be their weapons man and was a bomb expert. Bad guys with bombs were ATF's bread and butter, and I wanted to meet him in a bad way. She invited me out to her icehouse. Ice house, beer, meth head, and friend of the Bandidos…just another day in paradise. This was my life.

I drove out to the neighborhood in east Houston to meet her. The closer I got to the icehouse, the worse the neighborhood got. Burned out houses. Graffiti. Gangs. Abandoned cars and abandoned people. I drove up to an old, dilapidated house that looked like it was held together with one nail. All the windows had been busted out. Unsure, I looked again at the directions and sure enough, that house was the place. I walked up to the house, stepped on scattered, broken glass and walked inside the door-less clapboard cracker box.

There were a couple of tables, a few chairs, and some pretty mean-looking pit bulls drinking beer. They glanced over at me and snarled. I sat down alone with my back to the wall and watched. No females. This was the place, but where was the snitch? Suddenly, a woman screeched through the house as she chased a large, scrappy, nearly hairless cat. The butt and tail of a rat hung from its mouth. He chomped on it as fast as he could as that lady gained on him. She grabbed the cat and snapped that rat out of the cat's mouth, throwing the half eaten rat out the door. She yelled at the cat to get out, and sure enough, the cat leapt out the door as he chased the mangled half-eaten rat. She looked up and peered at me with those gizzards she had for eyeballs. Oh yeah, it was the lady I came to meet. I recognized that gravelly voice from the phone calls.

She said "hey" and walked over to the ice chest, popped the lid, reached in with her rat-snatching hand, and pulled me out a beer. Pabst Blue Ribbon. America's finest. She popped the lid and handed it to me, sat down, and started yapping about all of her problems. I had to steer her continually. I would have had better luck with a herd of cats. Finally, she focused. She said this biker dude used to be in

EOD in the military and went sideways. EOD meant Explosives Ordnance Detachment...the guys who took apart bombs. He was a white supremacist and now rode with the outlaws in the Bandido Motorcycle Gang. We agreed to meet that Friday night, and she would introduce me to this firecracker.

Late Friday night, I picked them both up, and we drove around Houston to shop for the components for a homemade bomb. We shopped at the twenty-four hour grocery store and the pharmacy for the components. They smoked dope. I faked it. After picking up all the bomb components, we went back to the biker's apartment and made five bombs. He thought I was a hit man and was going to kill a US attorney in Beaumont. I was only kidding. I really liked the US attorney in Beaumont.

Looking back, I guess he was kind of low-hanging fruit. He may have known how to make bombs, but he was no rocket scientist. Anyway, he made these bombs out of stuff that looked like bread dough when we were done with the process. He told me that this stuff was sensitive to shock and to handle it real careful like. He cradled the plastic bowl in his arms as he gently mixed the ingredients. I was amazed. The more this biker dude stirred the batch, the stiffer it got. He placed it on the table to steady it. He began to struggle as he mixed it up, and suddenly the bowl flew off the table and hit the kitchen cabinet. Everyone dove to the floor and covered their heads. I thought I was a dead man as I watched the bowl bounce around on the floor. Hmmm...nothing happened. It didn't go boom.

The biker reassured me that if I put a detonator in it, it would blow. He suggested that I put it in a container, place it outside of the US attorney's home on a windowsill, and shoot it when he walked by, causing it to detonate. Why not just shoot the US attorney as he walked past the window? Oh well, whatever. I didn't care if there was a better mousetrap. I just wanted this guy to do what he did best. Make a bomb. And wear bracelets.

I left with the bombs in my G-ride (my government issued vehicle) and dropped the snitch off at her home. I drove to my home clear on the other end of town and pulled into the garage. This was early Saturday morning. I went to work Monday and told my boss. He told me to do the paper (to write it up) and call the Houston Bomb Squad.

Now these bomb squad guys were all my buddies, and I had the utmost respect for them. Highly trained, top drawer. When they arrived, I walked them to the parking garage and opened the trunk. They asked me in great detail what we used to make the bombs. They asked me again, smiling a little at each other. I told them, and I think I told them again. They pulled the bombs out of the trunk and took them apart right there. They pulled out the bread dough and started laughing while throwing it all around in the parking garage.

I guess they thought it was pretty funny that the biker had tricked me into thinking the dough was explosive material. Just to be sure, I sent it to the lab.

I waited two weeks for the results. Turns out, this stuff used to be made in WWII by the US military and was used as some kind of high-impact explosive. I enjoyed reading the lab report over the phone to them. I could just see Ol' George the bomb tech turn pasty white, which he kind of was anyway.

I told you this little story to illustrate a point. Things are different now. Picking up a female snitch, alone, and driving around town with her is a big no-no today. Picking up a bad guy, no cover, meeting in his apartment, and making bombs would be big trouble for the modern agent. Driving around with both of them without surveillance, bringing the bombs home, and keeping the bombs over the weekend is a sure way to suspension today.

I really enjoyed my time with BATF and am grateful for the good times I experienced there. I must say that it was only the start of something greater for me. I was later hired by the Drug Enforcement Administration as a Special Agent and went on to have the greatest adventures of my lifetime.

WHITE MEN CAN'T BUY HEROIN

Lubbock, Texas was about a two and half hour drive south to Odessa, Texas. The DEA Resident office in Lubbock was responsible for the sister cities of Odessa and Midland but had no one assigned there. I volunteered to drive down there on the weekdays to work drugs.

Odessa and Midland sprung from the desert during the oil rush in the late 1800s. The management of the early oil companies populated Midland, located about twenty miles from Odessa, while Odessa reputedly became the home of the oil field workers. Over the last century, Odessa became known as a roughneck kind of town—full of corrupt politicians, prostitutes, and drugs. Midland, a more upscale town, enjoyed a more respectable reputation as a typical, all-American small town. The truth of it is I was lot more comfortable in Odessa. That may say something about me, but I really think the town was a good fit.

In order to get the lay of the land, I would drive down and meet with the local law enforcement to try and build bridges. Naturally, any time the federal government rolled in, there were preconceived notions. I mean, everyone trusts the government, right? Just ask the Native Americans. Mostly, their suspicions were correct, but I was not your normal Fed. Heck, I was just not normal by anyone's definition. I struck up some friendships, and of course, some enemies. It came with the job. This was their backyard, and a few didn't want anyone sniffing around.

Shortly after I introduced myself to the Narcs (narcotics agents) at the Narcotics Section of the Odessa Police Department, I brought with me one of the finest snitches I ever had to their office. This snitch would load up the heroin dealers on a commercial flight in El Paso bound for Lubbock with ounces of heroin stuffed in their shorts. I would pick them up at the airport, take them out to dinner, and then to the hotel to make the deal. I made a nice movie of the transaction, and to celebrate, we would award them with an Oscar, or because I was fresh out of Oscars, a pretty set of bracelets. Slam dunk. Over and over.

Sometimes this snitch would just send them up by car from El Paso, loaded with kilos of cocaine. I would meet them at the local hotel…make a movie…celebrate…then bracelets. What a snitch! I hardly had to work at it.

One day, the snitch called and said he knew some people in Odessa who dealt ounces of heroin. He knew one heroin doper well enough to introduce me. Hot dog…road trip! I drove to Odessa, picked up the snitch at the airport, and then drove with the snitch to the police department to meet with the Narcs. It turned out that the Narcs knew the target. The target was reputed to be from a large family of heroin dealers working in and around Odessa. They tried for many years to make buys on him, but were unsuccessful.

When I asked them to provide cover for me while I went in with the snitch, they flatly declared, "White men can't buy heroin." It had never been done before in Odessa, and they were not going to waste their time. The narcotics sergeant was very outspoken about this and insisted that they send in a Hispanic undercover officer to make the buy with my snitch. The deputy chief was a class act and respected the decisions of her subordinates. She supervised the Narcs and trusted their judgment. I had no problem with this and freely offered up my snitch to them so another agent could try and make a deal.

SWING AND A MISS

The Hispanic undercover officer met with the snitch and got their stories straight. We headed out on the operation, while I took a back seat and provided cover. I knew that the snitch was in capable hands and was very impressed with their tactical and surveillance skills.

Well, we didn't have to wait long. The snitch and the undercover walked up to the door, knocked, and were immediately rejected by the heroin dealer. Everyone split. We hooked up at the police department to talk to the undercover officer and debrief the snitch.

According to the snitch, the doper did not like to deal with anyone besides the snitch, but especially didn't like the undercover…it just didn't feel right to him. Well, I figured I wanted a shot at this, but knew if I failed I wouldn't hear the end of it. After all, everyone knows that white men can't buy heroin. The sergeant resisted, but the deputy chief overruled him. This did not sit well with the sergeant but he probably saw it as an opportunity to prove his point and throw a little egg on the out of towner's face (meaning me).

The snitch called the target and told him he had another buyer. This made it even tougher, as the snitch already had one bite of the apple and now begged for a second chance. We had a lot to overcome. I had a lot to overcome.

My great-great-grandfather was an Irish blockade-runner based in Charleston, South Carolina during the War of Northern Aggression. He escaped the Yankees by running his ship aground to set it on fire rather than let it fall into the hands of the Bluecoats. Maybe a little of his Irish luck rubbed off on me, because the heroin dealer agreed to a second meet.

This time we scheduled the meet in the parking lot of a mall to make a deal for a couple of ounces of heroin. With surveillance out of sight, the heroin dealer rolled up in his pickup and climbed into the front passenger seat of my G-ride. The snitch sat in the back seat and began to spin a tale about how he knew me and could vouch for me.

I told a few lies…attracted some flies…and he succumbed to my blarney. He handed me two ounces of heroin, and I knew then that all was good in the world. Life was beautiful. It was as if heaven itself opened up, and I could hear the angels sing.

The Narcs applauded my success. All but one. The sergeant was a little taken aback by this anomaly of a white man buying heroin, but he took it like a man.

FAMILY TREE

I went on to meet several members of this heroin-dealing family. Cousins. Uncles. It was a family affair. On one memorable late night, I met with two of them in a ramshackle trailer park in southeast Odessa to buy a few more ounces of heroin.

Alone as I waited in the dark, I saw two figures emerge from the shadows and walk up to me. We met. After a short discussion regarding the terms and the prospect of more dope in the future, they left to get the dope.

Thirty minutes passed before I got a call from the outside surveillance and was told the deal was called off. We met nearby, and I was told that there was a call over the police frequency for a unit to go to the same trailer park for an accidental shooting.

The two thugs I met with had returned to their trailer to pick up the heroin, and when they arrived, they found one of their relatives dead. He had picked up one of their guns and accidently shot himself. The entire family, thugs all, headed to the emergency room.

Though sorrowful for the senseless loss of life, I was by this time an old, crusty Narc and saw this as an opportunity. Now I know I shall pay a dear price for this in the next life, but I could not help but turn the event to my advantage. This family had supplied heroin to the downtrodden for generations. The destruction they had sown over the years had cut a wide swath of broken families and dead addicts. This had to end. Working dope has a nasty effect on your life as you learn to fight fire with fire, and this night I was going to set this deal on fire. I wanted to meet them all. All the dope-slinging members of this family. Every last one of them. What better opportunity than at the emergency room?

I asked the Narcs if they knew anyone with a flower shop. They did, and we went knocking on their door early in the morning. I walked out with an arm full of flowers and headed to the emergency room. The accident had been all over the media, and it would not be strange to them that I had heard about it.

I walked into the emergency room and found myself in the midst of a large family of dopers, distressed and saddened by the circumstances. I recognized the two I just met in the trailer park, walked over to them, and gave them my condolences and the mother of the victim, the flowers. They were visibly touched. They thanked me and introduced me to every one of their family members.

I had never seen so many thousand-dollar cowboy boots and silver belt buckles in one room before. I had hit the mother lode. I told them to call me when they could, but not to worry, I would be around. In one fell swoop I met the entire organization and gained their confidence. I know, I know. Don't say it.

I went on to make hand-to-hand buys with all of them, including the biggest victory of all, their source of supply, which proved my theory that white men can buy heroin…if they bring flowers.

CHAPTER THREE

ROUND 'EM UP, BOYS!

JOE THE RESTAURATEUR

There were rumors of a guy who lived in Hobbs, New Mexico who ran eighteen wheelers out to the Left Coast laden with two or three hundred kilos of cocaine. I was told that he was well connected and could put together a two-kilo coke deal in the Midland/Odessa, Texas area. My snitch said he could hook us up. Normally that would not be a problem, but the crook, Joe Gomez, was in an area that was not in my division. I was an agent in the Dallas Field Division who worked out of Lubbock, Texas. Hobbs, where Joe lived, was part of the El Paso Field Division, and it was a strict no-no to poach in their territory.

Not to pass up on a good doper, I kind of forgot about the strict guidelines for working deals in other folk's backyards. I really didn't want to wait around for El Paso's blessings. It kind of puts a drag on an investigation if you've got to jump through hoops. So I figured I would do the deal on the QT, and no one would be the wiser (or in the new youngster be-bop lingo, on the "down low").

My snitch convinced Joe to call me up. The snitch told Joe that I was a heavy hitter and hoped to expand my operation. I told Joe that I was a rancher from Lubbock and had a landing strip on my ranch. I explained to Joe that I was not happy with the people who sent me dope from Mexico and that I wanted to develop new sources I could depend on. Joe said that he was my man. He said he could get me two kilos of coke in Odessa from a buddy of his, and if the deal went well, I could get a lot more. This sounded pretty good to me, so I decided to go ahead and try to work out a deal with him.

I told Joe to meet me in Odessa, and we would drive over to the source's house. I should have gotten a clue about this guy from the get-go, because he said his truck was in the shop and I needed to pick him up and take him to Odessa. Now my little scheme to beat the paper needed to poach in New Mexico hit a snag. If I went to New Mexico to pick him up, I would have to have an entourage of cover agents, operation plans, air cover, permission to poach, two divisional chains of command to direct the operation, and a ton of paperwork. If I didn't do all this stuff and just drove to New Mexico, picking him up in stealth mode, I might get wacked by the bad guys, or worse yet, get in an accident in the G-ride—then I would really be toast.

So my decision boiled down to whether I should do it the hard way and risk the deal not going through, or do it the right way. It was an easy choice for me. I decided to do it the right way and lit out for Hobbs. It is easier to ask forgiveness than to ask permission only to be turned down.

Now there was the money to consider. It takes an act of Congress to get authorization to buy a kilo of cocaine, much less two. We're talking twenty thousand dollars each in 1993 dollars. (And for additional perspective, one kilo provides enough hits to put a sparkle in the eyes of at least five thousand druggies.) The more you buy, the cheaper it gets, but DEA didn't buy one or two kilos, unless, of course, it would lead to Jimmy Hoffa. But since Jimmy's dead, or in

Tahiti lying on some beach, odds were pretty good Joe didn't know him. So with the usual flare of a rogue agent, I planned to once again buy the dope with my shiny gold badge. (To "buy" the dope with a badge means to show them a badge and then bust 'em!)

On my way to Hobbs, I called my friends in Narcotics at the Odessa, Texas Police Department, told them my plan, and asked them to watch for me as I drove into Odessa with Joe. I stopped at home along the way and emptied out all the kids' toys and cop stuff. G-rides are for official use only...no kids. Never one to let a good rule go unbroken, I would cheat from time to time and drive my kids to school in my G-ride. They would leave their junk to roll around on the floorboard and stuffed under the seats, not to mention the candy wrappers and lollypops stuck on the floorboards. I always had to sterilize my G-ride before I went undercover or rode anywhere with a supervisor to make sure that no trace of my real life existed in my car.

I left Lubbock and headed out for Hobbs to pick up Joe. When I got to his house, I rolled up outside and honked my horn. Moments later, he peeked out of his door, walked outside, and climbed into my truck. He was a nice-looking guy about twenty-five years old. Clean-cut kid. He reached out to shake my hand and said that he had to get back by 6:00 pm for his kid's birthday party. I told him that it was up to him. If he hit a fast one in Odessa, we should make it.

As we drove to Odessa I massaged his brain with talk about my ranch, the tons of dope I moved, trust, integrity in the business, and how disappointed I was with all the goings on in the doper world. I moaned about missed deals, broken promises, and businessmen like myself who have to deal with coked-up hotheads. I hoped that one day I would share that kumbaya experience with a real doper, and we could grow old and make lots of money together. I was just flinging a lot of mud against the wall and hoped that something stuck. It was just a bunch of old school doper yarns. He listened and spun his own tale of deceit, telling me all about his big connections and how much stuff he could put on the table. He boasted about all the dope he ran to California. He said that this dude in Odessa was the man and could hook us up.

I asked Joe what he wanted out of this. He said he hoped to start a restaurant in Hobbs and needed some startup capital. He wanted to make enough over time with me to make it happen. I told him that if this guy in Odessa was consistent and could deliver eight to ten kilos a month, his dreams would come true.

POACHING WITH WEDGIE

As we drove up to the outskirts of Odessa, I picked up a tail. It was the Odessa Narcs. They followed us into Odessa and through the neighborhoods, undetected. We drove up to a small, non-descript cracker box home in a non-descript neighborhood, and I parked in front of the house on the street. Joe said the guy did not want to meet anyone and bolted from the truck for the front door. He knocked. Waited. Knocked again. Waited. Finally, a dirtball opened the door, looked at Joe, and slammed the door. Joe turned around and walked back to the truck. Got in. He looked like hammered dog doo-doo. I asked him what happened.

Moments passed. Without even turning his head, he mumbled, "This dude doesn't want to do the deal. He said that I owe him money and that he wants his scratch."

"Well, do you owe him, Joe?"

"Yeah, but I'm good for it. He should know that." He sat there for a moment. I thought he was going to cry, but then he snapped at me,

"Hey, could you front me the money? You can wait here while I go inside and get the dope."

Now I may be a hayseed from Texas, but I ain't a greenhorn. Never, ever…let me say that again…never, ever front the money. Only stupid people do that. Only stupid people or thieves ask that.

"Put your seatbelt on, Joe. We are going back to Hobbs." He started to act like he had a wedgie and got all fidgety.

"You can trust me—I won't rip you off. Just let me do this one deal. It'll work!"

I thought to myself, what kind of fool am I to drive all the way to Hobbs and risk suspension for this two-bit wannabe? I put the G-ride in drive and headed north to Hobbs. We made it a couple of blocks, and he said turn right. He said he knew another guy who could do a couple ounces. We started this trip talking kilos, and now we were down to ounces. What the heck? I figured, why waste the trip? I got all those Odessa Narcs in tow, and I figured a little road trip couldn't hurt. Besides, Narcs are used to caravanning around town to follow undercover guys shopping for dope. We drove to south Odessa and entered a trailer park.

Once again, Joe asked, "Could you front the money?"

I stuck to my guns. "Get out of the truck and get my dope!"

He looked upset when he jumped out of the truck and headed to the front door of the trailer. Knocked. Another slime ball answered the door and let Joe in. Minutes went by. Lots of minutes. I was just about to give up and contemplated leaving Joe there. As I put my truck in drive, Joe opened the door, slammed it, and left. He walked to my truck and got inside.

"You've got to front me the money or this guy won't give me the coke."

"We're going home, Joe. Buckle up." We headed north to Hobbs.

I called the Odessa Narcs from my mobile and cancelled the deal in code. Joe looked beat down. Things were real quiet all the way to Hobbs. Joe looked like someone just shot his dog. I told Joe not to worry about it, to stay in touch, and that maybe we could try some other time. He responded by asking me for fifty bucks to get his kid a birthday present. He must have known I had a soft spot for kids. I squeezed out fifty bucks from my wallet and handed it to him. Now, don't go thinking I'm getting squishy on you—I slowed down to thirty when I passed his house, and he did a tuck and roll out the door. My foot was planted firmly in his rear end.

I drove home a little ticked. Embarrassed that I drug out the Odessa Narcs on a false alarm but relieved that I was in stealth mode. No one in DEA knew where I was, so there was no explaining.

For the next year, Joe would call me on my mobile telling me about how he had not forgotten me and how he was going to come through. He talked about all kinds of dope deals. Nothing ever materialized. Everyone in the office told me that I was wasting my time…to blow off that mope. But the way I figured it, Joe believed in me. He thought I was a heavy hitter. Maybe someday he could make it happen. It became the office joke. I just blew the other guys off and told them to hold onto their hats. It could happen.

SHOPPING AT THE MALL

I did not hear from Joe for a while, and I figured he had given up. Then one day, out of the blue, he called me and said he had moved to Phoenix and was working at a car dealership.

"I met a guy here. He has family in Mexico who are in the business. From Sinaloa. You know…*the* Sinaloa." (He referred to the Sinaloa Cartel that now dominates drug trafficking in Mexico.)

"Uh huh. And this means what, Joe?"

"I know I've blown it, Tim, but this is for real."

"Sure it is, Joe."

Joe knew that he had failed in the past, but this time he promised it would happen. He just wouldn't quit. I started to think that he was stalking me.

"Look, Tim. They can do ten to fifteen (kilos) easy."

"Uh huh."

"Hey, they can do more if it goes smoothly." He began to chip away at my excuses. Maybe the memories of my past with Joe became a little bit fuzzy. Maybe I forgot just how cranky my boss got the last time Joe caused us some grief. Maybe I started to feel sorry for Joe. Nah, I think my change of heart happened because I smelled cocaine. While he jabbered about this stuff, my mind tried to figure out how I would jump through all those hoops to swing this deal in another division.

"Joe, I have been down this road before, and I'm not going to be dragged all the way to Phoenix for nothing. You've got to bring it to me."

"They won't let me, Tim. We can do it on the second deal. Please Tim," Joe begged.

I hesitated. Then I pulled the trigger. "Okay. I will be there tomorrow and meet you at a mall, but you had better come through. My people are getting real tired of you."

He was exhilarated and promised, "I won't let you down!"

Yeah, right. That's easy for him to say. I have to walk into my boss's office and explain to him why I want to fly to Phoenix and meet a guy who previously couldn't do two ounces of coke but could now get me fifteen kilos.

This may not seem like a big deal to a lot of people, but here is the run down: My boss calls his boss in Dallas. He tries to convince his boss that this deal can happen, conveniently leaving out all the failures in the past by this mope. If my boss's boss bites, then my boss's boss calls the boss in Phoenix and asks permission for me to fly out and do the dope deal. Now that may sound simple, but remember how it all went down in Hobbs? This would mean all the Phoenix agents would have to drop everything they are doing and babysit me.

This would tick off all the Phoenix agents, who have their own deals to work and have deadlines. If everyone agrees, which sometimes happens, then I have to write paper. Lots of paper, teletypes, and such. What a pain. All this in a couple of hours. If it all actually gets approved, I would then go home, pack, and fly out the next morning. The biggest lesson for a young narcotics agent to learn is that you have to "get through the good guys (management) to get to the bad guys."

I didn't know if it would all come together, but lo and behold, it did, and I flew out the next morning. It was Agent Kevin Carver who met me. Tall, good-looking, freckled Irish boy. He was a professional tennis player, BD (Before DEA). He left the pro life because he liked the regular paycheck. When I asked him how he got stuck on this deal with me, he told me he made the mistake of walking down the hallway in division holding a coffee cup and no folder. When he ran into the Assistant Agent in Charge (ASAC) of the Phoenix Field Division, Kevin looked up and the ASAC made eye contact with him. The ASAC looked down, stared at Kevin's coffee cup, and without skipping a beat, said he had a job for him. Kevin should have known better. Never walk around your office without a folder in your hand. Everybody knows that.

So I gave Kevin the run down, and he drove me to division. We met a bunch of agents who were waiting on me. They were nice enough considering I messed up their day. One guy stuck out as a really nice guy. Genuine. His name was Chuck Gulich. A dinosaur like myself. We became fast friends and kept our friendship over the years. As this case progressed, he watched my back, kept management at bay, and pulled my bacon out of the fire on more than one occasion. You will hear more about him later.

The agents gathered to formulate an operations plan for my undercover deal. I told them about my previous encounters with Joe, the crook, and I watched as many of their eyes rolled back into their sockets. I could read their minds as they asked themselves, "Who is this cowboy from Texas coming to our back yard and making flimsy, no-dope deals?" I knew it didn't look like a solid deal, but I had a feeling in my gut that if I followed through on this guy, it would come to life. Maybe. And of course, once again I would have to buy the dope with my badge or just thump him and take it.

With an ops plan in hand, we saddled up and headed to meet our bad guy. I had mapped out how everything was going to happen: Meet Joe at a nearby mall. Make talk. Joe wants to see money. I say no and call Joe stupid. Joe calls source. Source calls mule. Mule delivers dope. I arrest Joe and mule. Make Joe or mule talk, and they give up location of source. Run warrant on source's house. Seize more dope. Arrest source. Go home to a ticker-tape parade put on by my boss and fellow agents.

It sounded like a good plan, but all plans are perfect until you meet the enemy. This plan was no different. It actually went down like this: Met Joe. Made talk. Joe wants to see money. Called Joe stupid. Joe calls source. Source sent mule with fifteen kilos of cocaine. Time passes. One hour. Joe calls source. Two hours pass. No mule. Agents on surveillance ticked. I'm ticked. Three hours pass. No mule. No dope. Tell Joe never to call me again. I leave. No ticker-tape parade.

Once again, Joe blew it. I returned to the Phoenix Field Division office and thanked all the guys. Boy, they were not happy. I worked up the nerve to call the boss and give him the bad news. He was real good about it. Told me to wrap it up and come home, so I did.

When I came back, I expected the other agents to give me a hard time about it, especially since we were all in competition for our 13s. The big thing is getting your "13," meaning GS-13, Senior Agent status. It takes three to six years if you are lucky. The route to 13 varies from year to year as Uncle Sam continually moves the cheese. But this is not the point. To get your 13, you must have really good cases with really big targets, lots of conspirators, wiretaps, and complex intergalactic investigations. This is okay, but you have to be the only agent who gets credit for the case in order for it to count towards your 13. It cannot be shared with another agent. He has to get his own case with these qualifiers.

So how motivated is he to help you? Fortunately, most are willing to help because they love the job. But some agents love themselves and sit around throwing rocks at your stuff. They think there are only so many 13s to go around, so they figure if they make you look bad, it makes them look good.

In this warped way of looking at things, they believe that this improves their chances of getting their 13. So these guys love it when you fail to put dope on the table. They revel in it. Every office has at least one. When the boss walks down the hallway, he has to be careful so as not to get rear-ended by one of these guys if he slows down to make a turn. Get my drift?

So when I came back from Phoenix, needless to say, these meatballs had a heyday. I never heard the end of it. It was not one of my shinier moments on the job, and they wasted no time letting me know. My friends just chuckled with a "There but for the grace of God go I" attitude.

But like they always say, he who laughs last, laughs hardest.

PENANCE

Two weeks later, I got a call from my little dance partner, Joe. Yeah, I know. Don't say it. I have a soft heart. Or maybe a soft head. Fool me once…but three times? I don't know why I even answered the phone. I thought I had put that boy to rest with my final reports on the Phoenix fiasco. But as it turns out, that was only the beginning.

Joe called from a hotel room in Tucson.

"Tim? It's Joe. Don't hang up!"

"Well, if it isn't the man whose mouth writes checks that his body can't cash."

"Tim, I am really sorry—the dude got lost in traffic. He was from Mexico."

"Uh huh."

"No really; he was! He had the dope, man! Honest! Look, I got the vatos (dudes) from Mexico here now. They want to make it up to you. They feel really bad and…"

"Forget about it, Joe. I'll talk to you later."

"No, don't hang up!"

I let him ramble on about it and let him get out all his mea culpas so I could part on friendly terms. I really wanted to just reach through the phone and pull him through it to choke him out. He had caused me a lot of grief, paperwork, and embarrassment across two divisions.

"Tim, these vatos really do feel bad. They will get you all the white (cocaine) you want. I am right here with them in Tucson. In a hotel."

Well, I decided that I would bite. I had nothing else to do. Joe said he could get me any amount of cocaine I wanted. Just like that. Now I have heard this before from mopes (bottom-feeder dope dealers), drug addicts, and car salesmen. But never from some meatball who had failed to produce so much as a gram of powdered milk. I quietly listened to him as he rambled on. I thought I would play along just to see where it would lead me.

Now Joe thought I had this ranch with a landing strip, remember? I had led him to believe that the fifteen-kilo deal was only a test run for more to come. So the stage was set, but I was a mime. No props. I had to figure out a way to keep the fact that I did not have a ranch from Joe. If he brought it up, I would have to come up with a ranch and airstrip real fast.

"Okay, Joe. How much can these guys do?"

"Hold on." Joe held the phone to the side and I heard him speak Spanish to someone. They responded in Spanish, but I couldn't make out what they said.

"They can get you ANY amount you want."

"Quit jerking me around Joe!"

"No really Tim—ANY amount."

"Okay, I'll bite. I want five hundred kilos." This was followed by a moment of silence. I heard voices in the background as Joe talked to the vatos. Joe's voice got real serious when he responded.

"How often do you want it?"

"Don't blow smoke at me."

"It's the real thing, Tim."

"Don't make promises you can't keep, Joe. My people have very little patience and don't like being jacked around. They are kind of like the Mafia," I responded and silently added in my head, "or even worse, DEA supervisors."

"Tim, these guys are heavy hitters. They will do this. How often?"

"Every three days." Yeah, I know. I said it. What idiot would believe that anyone could actually supply or even move that much dope?

I figured Joe was in a fantasyland, and I wanted to play too. While I waited, Joe machine-gunned Spanish to the toads in the room. I heard jabber back and forth in Spanish and realized that there were probably at least three more guys in the room. Joe got back on the horn.

"No problemo."

"Joe, I want you to understand what I am saying. That's five hundred kilos every three days. Five thousand kilos a month. Right?"

He hammered back that he knew what I wanted and asked me when I was going to come to Tucson.

"Whoa there! I ain't going anywhere, Joe!"

Joe moved a little too fast. I wasn't going anywhere. There was no way, no how, my bosses were going to let me go back to Phoenix, I thought to myself. Not after the last deal. If I thought that I was taking hits for the Phoenix deal now, wait until I tell them that Joe promised me five hundred kilos! Every three days! Oh yeah. Sure. That was going to go over really well.

"They are going to have to come to Lubbock."

It was obvious that this was understandable considering how they left me hanging the last time. I used this to my advantage and pressed Joe to deliver the dope to Lubbock. They told Joe that they would not, or could not—I wasn't sure which one it was. Joe then announced, "They want $22,000 dollars a kilo."

"Goodbye, Joe."

He jumped and said, "Wait! $22,000 is only a starting point!"

"No, Joe, that is the finishing point."

What kind of fool did they think I was? Only a cop would say yes. I was a businessman, or so they thought, and I was going to get the best price I could for Uncle Sam.

"I'll pay fifteen."

Joe chuckled and shot back, "I'm not even going to tell them that."

I told him that I bought a lot of dope and, if they would not work with me, I would go down the street and hook up with someone else. I also said the Columbians were doing it for less than they were asking, delivered to New York. (I had never met a Columbian, but it sounded really cool.) It was like going to a garage sale. We went back and forth—yelling, crying, and squeezing till I got them down to $17,000 a key. A heck of a deal. My dad would have been proud.

The only hitch was that I had to come up with the money. Have I mentioned that DEA doesn't spend a lot of money to buy dope? I figured it would be too much to ask for the $85,000,000 a month, or just $8,500,000 every three days. So I decided that the every three-day option was more workable (you know, spread out the payments). But considering the fact that I was going to pay for it with my badge made it seem all the more achievable. I love carrying a badge: you can shop anywhere the dirtballs are selling their wares and when they say, "Show me the money," I show them my badge, and they go for a ride to meet Bubba at Club Fed.

But there was another small problem.

"They want to see the money, Tim."

"Joe, I traveled all the way to Phoenix with my money the last time, and they blew it. I'm not going down that road again!"

But Joe insisted that they wanted to see the money first. There we went again! What was it with the money thing? How come they always want to see the money? How come I can't see the dope first? Why is it always about them? At this point, we got stuck in the mud. They would not come out, and I would not saddle up.

I figured the only way I would convince my people to allow me to go on this road trip was to have a sample of the dope they peddled. DEA had to be sold on the idea that it could happen before I had their blessings to travel.

Now normally, a sample is a very small amount of dope, which the doper gives you to test for purity—a gram, or even an ounce in a large deal. The operative term here is "gives." Free. Big dopers (like Joe and his cohorts believed me to be) and DEA do not pay for samples. With the way things were going, I would not even be able to pull $200 from the PE/PI fund on this dead horse. (PE/PI is the fund we used to "Purchase Evidence/Purchase Information.") So I thought I would make them put their money where their mouth was.

"Joe, if you want me out there, you've gotta bring me a kilo sample. Gratis."

That was twenty thousand dollars' worth of cocaine, free. Unheard of. I figured if they were for real, they could do this, and I could go on a road trip. There was dead silence on Joe's phone. Moments later, I heard voices in the background. Very brief. Joe spoke up.

"When do you want it?"

It was Friday. I told him the sooner he could get here, the sooner I could come. He said he would drive to Hobbs Saturday, spend Sunday with his family, and drive north to Lubbock to deliver the kilo.

I reminded him, "I'm not paying for the dope."

"Yeah, I remember. But you've got to come to Tucson on Tuesday to meet my people. These dudes are big shots in Mexico, and they won't be happy if you don't come."

It was more of a warning than a comment about pleasing them. If it was true, and Joe delivered, I knew it would be the big one—bigger than anything I had ever done before—so I agreed.

I told Joe to go the intersection of 50th Street and University in Lubbock, Texas and pull up next to an ATM machine. I would meet him there and take the kilo. He agreed. We hung up, and I contemplated what had just transpired. Could Joe have done it this time? He certainly believed in the people in the hotel room. It couldn't be a rip (robbery) because I told Joe I would not pay for the sample. He knew I would not have any money with me. I started to believe that it really could happen, but I wasn't going to tell anyone. If Joe blew it, no one would know. My plan was to take delivery alone. That way when Joe failed, I could go on with my life, as if nothing happened.

MAKE MY DAY, JOE

It was a stroke of genius. Sometimes I really impress myself. On the southeast corner of this intersection was the DEA office. DEA had no sign outside. It just looked just like any non-descript office building. In the parking lot was the ATM machine where Joe was to meet me.

Beside my desk in the office was a window that overlooked the parking lot with the ATM. On Sunday morning, I set up the video camera beside my desk, pointed out the window towards the ATM and waited for Joe's call that he was en route from Hobbs, NM. He called. His voice was tight, serious. I knew he was in the zone. For the first time I believed that it could happen. I waited and watched outside for him to drive up. A few hours later, at dusk, he arrived and parked beside the ATM machine in the parking lot. I turned on the video camera and walked from the rear of the building parking area and across the parking lot to Joe's car. He glanced over at me and chirped, "Hey, Tim!"

He opened his truck and handed me a package, which contained a kilo of cocaine. There is this feeling that comes over you when you realize you've got your guy. At that moment, I knew. Joe and I were about to go on an adventure, only he would not be happy about the end game. He believed that this was the beginning of his future, his restaurant in Hobbs. He, too, felt like we were now joined at the hip.

It had been a long, bumpy road from the beginning. But now it was our time to put together the mother of all dope deals with my little buddy Joe, the Restaurateur. We made a nice couple.

I waved as Joe drove off and promised to call him when I got in town on Tuesday. As his vehicle drove out of my sight, I could hardly stand it. I bolted for the office and ran to my desk. I shut down the video and laid the package on the desk. Opened it. There before my eyes was a vision of loveliness, a pristine white cake of cocaine about the size of a tissue box. I felt like all my work on this meatball had finally paid off, and I could not wait to walk in the office on Monday to share my good fortune with all the "I told ya so" Monday morning quarterbacks. Hot diggity dog.

I woke up early Monday morning feeling all frisky. I rushed around while I packed up for the trip and dashed to the office to update my supervisor. I could not wait to see the look on his face.

I guess I expected a little too much from my boss when I walked in and told him I met Joe this weekend. I stopped short in my announcement when I saw something in his eyes that warned me that he was about to go where all of my previous supervisors had gone before. At some point in their working relationship with me, my supervisors invariably went through "The Five Stages of Grief." I could see him working through them as I stood there and watched his eyes glaze over. First, denial: "I told him to blow off that mutt, Joe. It's like he can't even hear my instructions. Maybe all that practice at the shooting range is hurting his hearing. I think I'll schedule him for a hearing examination. Yeah, I think that'll help." Without fail, anger quickly followed: "I wonder if the Phoenix Field Division needs an extra agent, because I don't need blood on my hands this close to retirement." Next came the bargaining. "Please God, I'll never use my G-ride to pick up the ladies again, just make him go away!"

When the bargaining didn't work, depression always followed.

During this stage, he usually sat on the verge of tears pining away for the days before I arrived, soothing his turbulent emotions with cake as he mumbled, "Leave me alone, Sellers. I just want to eat my cake." And finally acceptance: "You know, Sellers doesn't color within the lines, but I've got to admit, he's a great agent." I saw that this final stage of grief, acceptance, had blossomed when I dropped that kilo of cocaine on his desk with a loud, celebratory thud.

SEVENTY-FIVE BUCKS

Sure enough, I found myself on an airplane headed back to Phoenix on Tuesday. Kevin Carver met me at the airport, and we drove southwest to Tucson. He said everyone in the Tucson office was on hold for us. When we arrived, he took me around and introduced me to the bosses. After I paid homage to the Supremes, we walked to the undercover phone, and I made the call announcing my arrival to Joe the Restaurateur. He answered the phone and said he was with the big boys in room 150 at the Pueblo Inn. Joe said that he would introduce me to the boys from Mexico at the hotel. After we reached an agreement, they would drive me out to see the first five hundred kilos. I told Joe that I was not going to show any money until I saw the dope. Joe said they were on board with that, so I told him I was ready to meet.

I updated the gathered Tucson agents, and we finalized the operation plan. The agents would set up a perimeter around the Pueblo Inn and follow us to the stash location following negotiations. We decided on a verbal signal for them to come in with guns blazing if things went south. It was impossible to give a visual signal, as I was on the bad guys' turf, inside of a hotel room and out of sight. We had to rely upon the verbal for my danger signal. This was only viable if the hidden transmitter I wore worked. I told them that if the transmitter failed, which is not unusual, I would call them from the hotel phone every thirty minutes under the guise of updating my partner who was holding the money. If they did not hear from me at the appointed time, they should mount up and crash the door. But by then it may be too late. When these things blow up, they flame out pretty quickly. But there was no other choice but to call off the deal, which I was not going to do. I had to play this out.

I drove up to the hotel in my rented black Lincoln Continental with my boots, lid, and a big gun stuffed in my backside. I got out of the rental car and walked into the lobby and met with Geraldo Primo. Joe told me that Geraldo was related to the players from Mexico and that Joe and Geraldo worked together at the car dealership in Phoenix. Geraldo was a little round guy with a friendly face. He didn't speak a word of English. Together we walked to room 150, which was an interior room. It was impossible for the outside agents to visually monitor, so I was on my own.

Geraldo knocked on the door, and Joe opened the door to invite me in. It was 4:30 pm. I looked around the room and saw a guy sitting on one of two double beds. Joe introduced me to him as the main man. His name was Luis Gabaldon. This guy looked like a normal kind of guy, besides his glassy eyes, which gave me a feeling of foreboding. But all in all, he didn't look like a man capable of dealing millions of dollars' worth of dope every month. You had to be pretty rough to fight your way to the top of a goldmine like that, but from where I stood, Luis didn't look the part. Joe served as translator. Now, I know a little Spanish, enough to know when things are not going my way and when things are. I also had that "hair up on the back of your neck" thing that all cops have. With that and my little knowledge of Spanish, I felt like I could read these guys pretty well. I understood more than they realized, and this was a good thing.

Luis took a while to warm up to me. I think he was sizing me up as well. He said he was sorry for the failure to deliver the fifteen kilos of cocaine in Phoenix earlier and confirmed what Joe had told me. Luis told me through Joe that his people were not happy with the price. Now they wanted $19,000 a kilo. I could see that they were getting a little greedy. What is a couple of million or three when you are talking $85,000,000 or so a month? Well, there were two ways of looking at this: either I give in like a cop pretending to be a doper because I ain't paying for it anyway, or I act like a real doper and scream to high heaven about how they brought me all the way from Texas just to yank me around. It was an easy choice. I lit 'em up and shamed them for having gone back on their word and disappointing me. I told them that if this was how they were going to do business, it did not bode well for our continued relationship.

We settled on the original price of $17,000 per kilo. This was $8,500,000, which oddly enough was exactly what I brought with me! (I really only had $75 in my pocket. I was a little short that month, as my kids needed school supplies.) Luis said he could deliver it every four to five days without difficulty and after a while, get it out every three days. I figured that was close enough to the previously agreed upon delivery time of three days and didn't squawk about it. The timing didn't matter anyway if this ended how I hoped it would—no one can move dope from jail.

Luis added that if I would fly into Mexico and pick up the dope, he would give me a much better price. He assured me that all of the Mexican law enforcement and military were paid off and would not interfere. I told him that I would not fly to Mexico, but could possibly send my emissaries. All the finer points of negotiation worked out, Luis moved on to what he was really after: the cash. He said that he now wanted me to bring the money to the hotel so that he could look at it.

My expression didn't reveal the jolt I felt at this little turn of events. Trying to figure out what was going on, I looked at Joe and Joe innocently looked back at me, like "Gee, didn't you know this was coming?" His face froze, trying to hide the fact that he lied about the money. He apparently told Luis that I would show the money first to get them to come. What a scammer. Not that it made a difference. Either way, it always came down to this: you show me yours first and then I will show you mine. Why would I expect anything else?

I lit into Joe, "Now listen and listen good, Joe! It wasn't that long ago that I brought my money all the way to Phoenix from Lubbock, Texas. I showed up with my money. Where was your dope?" (I left out the fact that I never showed him my money and knew that he probably lied to Luis and the boys about seeing the money to convince them I was the real thing.) "You've only shown me one kilo. I have nearly $9,000,000 invested in this deal and you only have one kilo. My $9,000,000 cost me more than your one kilo. I'm not going to risk getting ripped! Show me the dope or I walk."

Joe said something in Spanish to Luis, and Luis caved. The deal was moving forward.

TOO MANY CHIEFS

Geraldo walked in and out of the hotel room during this heated discussion. I knew there was someone else close by that he was apparently updating. I began to realize that maybe Luis was not the lead in this deal. I asked him if he had the authority to conduct these negotiations. He assured me that he did but that he was also considering the desires of his partners, who were nearby. Luis emphasized that he was the only one responsible for making agreements of this magnitude. He said that he would take me to a nearby residence in Tucson after he made arrangements to move the dope from the stash location, which was a small ranchito (ranch) outside of town.

Things calmed down a bit, and I told the droolers in the room that I had to call my partner Kevin—the "moneyman"—and tell him to prepare the money to move on my instruction. In my phone call to Kevin, I made sure he understood that things were going well. He then warned me that my transmitter was intermittent and that I should continue to call to let them know everything was okay. I hung up and told Luis that my boy was ready. Before Joe could finish his translation of what I said, the hotel room door opened and in walked another dude.

Joe introduced him to me as Guillermo. He was later identified as Fernando Alarcon. Fernando is what I'll call him, since that was his real name, and Guillermo is too hard to pronounce. Fernando walked over to Luis and spoke briefly with him. Then he turned to me and said that he wanted to see the money. What was up with this guy? I couldn't keep everyone straight! I asked them who was in charge. Joe? Geraldo? Luis? Fernando? I started to get a little agitated and Fernando knew it. Luis and Joe became a little twitchy too.

Fernando explained that there were four partners in charge, but that both he and Luis had the authority to make the deal. I thought to myself, "He said four, so who else is coming?" Fernando apologized and agreed to the terms, restating the agreement. Fernando told Luis to telephone the stash location to make arrangements to move five hundred kilograms to a home in Tucson. I did not hear any specific locations. I called Kevin from the hotel phone again to tell him to get the money ready to move and signaled things were okay. Kevin said the sound was dead because the wire transmitter I wore went down and asked if I wanted to risk it. Were there cows in Texas? I wanted to take this train as far as it would take me.

I noticed that Fernando started to look me over real good. I could tell that he appeared more street-wise than the others. Suddenly, he waved to the others to follow him out of the hotel room. Everyone but me. I was stuck in the room alone, unsure why they left so quickly. I debated whether I should call for back up. Were they going to come back in with guns blazing? Or did they figure out that I was a cop and ran for their lives? For the life of me, I did not know why they left. Five minutes went by and suddenly the door opened and in walked Joe.

Joe was visibly upset and shaken. He said that Fernando saw my gun stuck in my backside (it was hard to miss) and was not happy. He reminded me that we all agreed not to carry any guns. Well now, I had heard about guys who never carried guns when they went undercover, in fear that the bad guys might find one. But I ain't one of those guys. I guess I would rather shoot my way out than talk my way out.

I told Joe that I was by myself with four—maybe five—guys making a multi-million dollar dope deal. I didn't think the odds were in my favor, and I needed an equalizer. Joe said that they were going to call off the deal if I did not get rid of the gun. Well, I had no guarantee that if I got rid of my gun, that they wouldn't have one. But I figured I wanted that dope deal pretty bad. That is the biggest mistake an undercover agent makes. He wants the dope so bad that he presses on and ignores the risks that come when rules are changed. Rule number one—never give up your gun. Rule number two—never give up your gun. Rule number three—give up only one gun. I had another that they did not know about. It was a five shot wheel gun stuck in my crotch.

I told Joe that it was cool with me if I had his assurances that they had no guns. Of course, he said they did not. (And I believe in unicorns and leprechauns.) I told Joe that was good enough for me and asked him to walk me to my car. We left the room and walked to my Lincoln in the parking lot. I opened the trunk and pulled my Sig Sauer pistol from my backside and placed it on the floor. Closing the trunk, I handed Joe the keys and said, "Let's go make some money." We walked back to the room, and I walked in alone.

Joe continued on to meet the others. They all returned and looked very serious. Joe told me it was okay and that they were ready to go. Luis telephoned another person staying in the hotel. Within five minutes, a person later identified as Benito Ramiro arrived in the room. I started to think that there must have been a doper convention in town and that everyone wanted to have happy hour in our hotel room. Here I am with five guys, one gun with five bullets, and no pizza. So I ordered up some pizza. No one wants five, cranky dope dealers on their hands.

While Fernando and Luis took turns calling the ranchito, Benito and I got to know each other. He was a clean-cut, good-looking guy. Very dapper. He said he was in charge of the money in Mexico and was really interested in how I laundered my money in the United States.

I went on and on about real estate and such, talking about all the ways I hid my money from detection. Blabber, blabber. Pizza came. We stuffed ourselves. I got a little bored as we waited for the dope to get moved. I think we all were, except for Fernando, who was stressing on the phone.

At 6:30 pm, Fernando left the hotel room to help in the movement of the five hundred kilograms of cocaine. Luis told me that his people had over one ton of cocaine at their stash house, a ranch fifteen to twenty minutes west of Tucson. Luis said they were having problems loading five hundred kilograms of cocaine on a vehicle that would not show displacement. Five hundred kilos would make any car or truck look like a low rider and attract the attention of cops.

Both Luis and Geraldo tried to reassure me that the deal was going to go down that evening. Hours passed. At 9:50 pm, I told them I was not going to wait any longer and left with instructions for them to call me if they could get it together. At 10:30 pm, I called Joe at the hotel and asked him if there was any progress. Joe said that they would deliver one hundred kilos in the morning and four hundred more kilos in the afternoon. I agreed. Pigs get fat, hogs get slaughtered.

JIM

We were up early the next day. I sought out the tech agents to get a hold of the tape recordings from the night before. I hoped to have at least a portion of the recordings before the wire I had worn went down. When I asked them for the tapes, they told me that they hadn't even bothered to record it. I learned later that no one had any confidence that my deal was going to go down.

Considering Joe's track record, I guess I couldn't blame them. At least they kept the sound up as long as they could for my safety. This played an important role later, as one of the defense attorneys cried foul because of the lack of recordings. The public believes that the government can track a bear's rear end in Alaska via satellite, so why can't we have video ready for the five o'clock news?

I met Kevin at the office and called Joe from the undercover phone at 8:00 am. Joe said he would check on it. At 11:30 am, I called Joe again and asked if he knew anything. Joe said that Fernando had overslept, but that he was en route to the stash location to ensure the delivery this morning. I told Joe to make sure the dope was there and to look at it before he arranged a meet. At 3:30 pm, Joe said they had just returned from the residence. The residence was only five minutes from the hotel on the 2800 block of Wagon Wheel in Tucson.

Joe said he saw the cocaine in the trunk of a white Ford Thunderbird parked in the garage. I told him I would come by with the moneyman, Kevin, but no money. When I saw the cocaine, I would order up the dough. Kevin and I told the agents on standby that the deal was a go.

We did not have an address, but knew it was a short drive to the house where the dope was. The cover agents had to follow us and listen in on the wire to find the house. This meant I had to drive slow and not make any sudden turns while I sent them coded messages of our location over the wire transmitter.

An inexperienced agent was in charge of the raid operation in the field. It was her job to decide when to go in and hit the house. She also had to decide if she needed to pull Kevin and me out if things went south before I gave the bust signal. Chuck Gulich was on the entry team and also monitored the wire.

I left to pick up Joe, Luis, and Geraldo at the hotel. We loaded up in my Lincoln and drove to the Wagon Wheel residence. We arrived at 4:25 pm. Surprisingly, it was a nice place, in a good neighborhood. Kevin and I walked in with the others. I immediately observed a pretty mean-looking dude who sat in a chair to the right of the door in the living room. Joe introduced him as "Joe" (no relation to my buddy Joe). We identified him as Jose Castillo. A real bad guy. I knew by looking in his eyes that he was there to protect the dope. He had that look of evil in his eyes; no mistaking this guy for anything else but death eating a cracker. I knew that when things went south, this dude was going to be in the mix.

Fernando was already at the house. Hail, hail, the gang's all here.

I was already making a body count for stats. Luis walked us over towards the kitchen and introduced "Jesus" (no relation to the Jesus of world renown). Luis said that Jesus and Jose had come in from Mexico for this deal. Luis escorted Kevin and me as he followed Fernando and Joe into the front bedroom. They didn't waste any time.

Fernando opened the closet and we saw two large green plastic bags stuffed with multiple kilograms of cocaine. I had no idea how much was there, but I knew it was enough to send these boys away for a long time. I pulled out two brown tape-wrapped bricks of cocaine and laid them on the floor. Things were real tense. Jesus walked in and began to talk with Fernando. Luis left.

I asked Fernando how often and how much they could be depended upon to deliver. Joe translated his response. Fernando said that if it all went well, he would arrange for Kevin and me to pick up by air five hundred kilograms of cocaine at their ranch in Mexico every two days instead of three, which meant that I no longer dealt with an $85,000,000 dope deal—I now looked at a $125,000,000 deal, but who's counting? Jesus said that they had already greased the skids with the cops and military in Mexico. Okay, I liked it. Mucho mas dopo. Now we were talking. The mother of all dope deals, and all I had was about ten dollars in my pocket as I'd already blown sixty-five on pizza and stuff. Boy, were they gonna be ticked.

Kevin left the room with Joe to get the test kit. As Kevin walked to the car with Joe, Joe told him that we had better be for real, because these guys were killers, and they wanted to see the money before we got any more dope. I knew the jig was up. No more dope without dinero, and these guys were getting antsy. It was time to call in the cavalry, or we were going to go hostage or take a dirt nap.

When Kevin returned and was testing the dope, I gave the bust signal. I thank God that my transmitter was working that day. The bust signal was my telling Kevin "Jim was really going to like this dope." While we waited for the cavalry, Kevin pulled out a mayonnaise bottle of bleach from a bag and cut a sample out of one of the bricks. He dropped the sample in to the bottle and waited for the cut to drop in the bleach, leaving the cocaine to float on the top. I don't know if this works, but it looks really cool. They were all watching the cut sink to the bottom of the jar as Kevin and I exclaimed that it looked good. Joe looked relieved.

Suddenly we all heard a crashing at the front door and voices yelling, "DEA! Get on the floor!" I looked into the fear-struck faces of Jesus, Fernando, and Joe and knew if the agents did not come through that door now, we were in for a fight. A young agent rushed into the bedroom with his sub-machine gun as he screamed for everyone to get on the floor. Fernando leapt to the window and I tackled him, wrestling him to the ground. Jesus dropped to the floor. Joe was in shock, looking at me as he slowly dropped and sobbed out loud that he believed in me. He repeated it over and over. I had crushed his spirit. He lay on the floor like a pile of warm spaghetti.

Everyone in the house was arrested. Seven in total. We counted the bricks of cocaine and found only forty kilograms. I asked Joe where the rest of the dope was. He stared blankly at me. I told him that now was the time to make a deal, not later. He hesitated and whispered that another sixty kilos was en route and would arrive in a white T-Bird. We called out to the cover team on the outside, told them to pull back and await the arrival of the T-Bird, and we hunkered down inside, securing the prisoners, weapons, and dope. Sure enough, within a short time, a white T-Bird lumbered up Wagon Wheel and turned into the driveway. Agents blocked off the T-Bird from escape and arrested Israel Alvarez, a former Mexican police officer. Alvarez made it eight defendants in total. Inside the trunk of the vehicle were sixty more kilos of cocaine. It was over without a hitch.

I learned later that the agent in charge of the operation called the big boss and complained that Chuck had jumped the gun, essentially dumping Chuck in the grease. She never heard the bust signal and was angry that Chuck ordered the troops in against her demands to hold. Chuck, of course, heard the bust signal I gave and led the raid team against her warnings to hold. When I heard of this, I called her aside and told her that I gave the bust signal and was real glad Chuck came in when he did. That ended it.

I took Joe the Restaurateur to a private room in the house and told him that I would do what I could to help him if he told us where the rest of the dope was. He said that they had the rest on a ranch outside of Tucson, but that he had not been there personally. He added that they had planned to bring it in the T-Bird, a hundred pounds at a time, after I showed them the money. They sure were hung up on me paying for that stuff.

I called my boss in Lubbock and told him about the success of the dope deal, and he was real happy. The boys in Phoenix called me the "King Kong" of undercover, which was a big about-face from the names they called me the last time I tried to do a deal in their neighborhood. The teletype put out by Phoenix Field Division Office went worldwide to every office in DEA and stated "...the unique undercover techniques demonstrated by Special Agents Sellers and Carver deserve special recognition." If unique could be described as showing up at an $85,000,000 dope deal with $75 in my pocket, then I guess they were right.

TACO STAND

The trial came a year later. Over the year, I met with Joe at the US Attorney's Office several times. The US attorney is the federal prosecutor. Joe offered corroboration on all the players, and I hoped that he would get as little as five to seven years in the federal penitentiary rather than the twenty-five to twenty-seven years he was probably going to get. It was not my decision what his penance would be, but up to the federal judge. Joe signed an agreement with the US attorney. He agreed to be honest with his corroboration and testimony, and in return, the US attorney would recommend leniency to the federal judge after the trial of the defendants.

Things rocked along. Seven of the defendants were convicted and sentenced from twenty-three to twenty-seven years in the federal pen. The eighth defendant, "Jesus," argued for a separate trial, and it was granted.

I flew to Phoenix for the trial and went to the US Marshal's office to pick up Joe. When Joe and I entered the elevator, Joe would not look at me.

I kinda smiled and said, "You look like someone just shot your dog. You okay?"

He just kept staring down at his cuffed hands and mumbled, "They needed the money."

"Who needed the money, Joe?"

Joe didn't move, and quietly said, "My wife and kids...they needed it."

I was getting impatient with him and raised my voice asking, "What are you talking about?"

"Jesus gave me thirty grand to lie about him. To cover for him."

I couldn't believe my ears. I snapped at him, "You're a fool, Joe. Don't do it!"

Joe quietly responded, "It's too late. My family already has the money. I'm sorry."

Phoenix DEA should have expended a little effort to keep them apart, but it probably wouldn't have made a difference. Jesus would have got to him no matter where he was. He needed Joe.

Jesus' excuse for his presence the day of the bust was that he owned a small seafood restaurant in Mexico and was in Tucson to house-sit the home on Wagon Wheel for the owner. Unbeknownst to him, all of these people showed up and suddenly he was caught up in a dope deal.

Joe sat there on the stand and lied, corroborating Jesus' testimony. I sat there and watched Joe. He avoided eye contact with me, and it was over. (Joe paid dearly for this. Following the trial, we had a hearing regarding the agreement the US attorney had with Joe. I testified about his failure to live up to the agreement, the conversation in the elevator, and the perjury he committed on the stand. The judge revoked the agreement. Joe was later sentenced to serve roughly twenty-five years. The $30,000 bribe came out to about $1200 for every year that Joe had to serve for helping Jesus. I'd say that's a poor-paying gig.)

As for Jesus, Joe's lies coupled with the fact that we did not have any videos of the drug deal caused enough doubt in the minds of the jurors. (They did not consider the fact that we did the negotiations and the delivery of the dope in the dopers' hotel room and their home, which made it impossible to video record the event.) They decided in favor of the defense and found Jesus not guilty. To say that this was a disappointment is an understatement. I had testified that I stood in the room with Jesus and the cocaine and that I conversed with him about this dope and future deals. They were unaware that all of the co-defendants were convicted and sent away essentially for life. The jury would not even make eye contact with me when they filed out of the courtroom. It only takes one juror to exonerate. Was it only one? If there were more, I will never know.

Either Joe or the lack of technical support to prove the case failed to find Jesus guilty beyond a reasonable doubt. But I began to wonder if Jesus reached out and touched someone on the jury like he did Joe. We were prevented from discussing the bribe in front of the jury, so they had no reason to suspect it themselves. It seemed that the testimony of a federal agent, along with the fact that the cocaine was found at Jesus' feet when he was arrested was not enough for the jury to find the defendant guilty.

Many years later, I visited Joe the Restaurateur in the federal penitentiary in Big Spring, Texas. He had sent word that he wanted to talk with me. Joe offered to work off some of his time for some intelligence on some dope dealers in Mexico. All of his intelligence was time stamped and expired. I could not help but gloat a little. I reminded him of his perjury and that he had sold his life for $1200 a year.

The last I heard, in 2002 or so, Joe wrote a letter to the US attorney in Albuquerque complaining that the government broke its original agreement. After a thorough investigation, it was dismissed. Joe will get out when I am in my sixties. Joe the Restaurateur. Maybe I can go see him at his Taco Stand when he gets out of jail. Or not.

CHAPTER FOUR

HARD TIMES

OKC

I was at home when I first heard that an explosion occurred at our DEA Oklahoma City Resident Office. DEA operated out of the ninth floor in the Alfred P. Murrah Federal Building in downtown Oklahoma City and reported to the Dallas Field Division. At the time of the explosion, I worked at the Lubbock, Texas Resident Office, and we also reported to the Dallas Field Division.

I rushed to the office and found everyone standing around while they watched it on television and simultaneously burned up the phone lines. We were all in shock. We knew everyone up there and hoped that they made it out of the building. The visuals on television did not offer much hope.

The explosion occurred at exactly 9:02 am. That was about the time most agents rolled into the office due to late night hours. But many others—office assistants, clerical, and related positions—were always there by 8:30 am. The devastating explosion made the building look as if the entire inside structure was gutted. Hundreds of federal employees worked in this building. There was even a daycare there used by the federal workers. It looked bad—real bad.

Fearing the worst, we each went home and packed up, making

preparations to go. We were told to be ready and await orders from division to head up to Oklahoma. We spent the entire morning prepping and making arrangements to spend a lot of time in Oklahoma. We expected to receive the call at any moment. It didn't come till that night.

We lit out early in a caravan of six G-rides going a hundred miles an hour northeast to Oklahoma City (OKC). What was normally a six-hour drive, we did in four. We rolled into OKC in the morning. The cars in the parking lot across from the federal building still smoldered. Seeing the bombed-out building firsthand was beyond anything one could imagine. There was a large crater where the rental truck had parked when it exploded, ripping out the innards of the building and collapsing all the floors, one on top of the other. The effects of the explosion left a crescent of each floor intact in the upper levels, forty feet wide on one side and dwindling to a few feet of floor as it wrapped around the inside of the upper floors that clung to the exterior wall.

Along the edges of each remnant of flooring were large broken sheets of concrete that dangled by rebar that had been imbedded during the construction of the building. They were weighted guillotines or "widow makers" that hung over the heads of rescue workers who scurried about the rubble as they looked for any signs of life. One large section of dangling concrete loomed above, threatening to fall onto the rescue workers and crash through the rubble to the parking garage beneath the building. It had its own name—they called that one the "Mother Slab."

While efforts were made to cut off the hanging chunks of concrete, they ordered the rescue workers off the rubble. We took this time to check into the hotel. After checking in, we headed back over to the bombsite and joined the other rescue workers. When all the hanging concrete was removed (the "Mother Slab" remained, due to its size and damage it would cause to cut it down), everyone climbed back onto the rubble and began passing pieces of the blown-out building down to more workers, who stacked it to the side for its removal to another site for the FBI Evidence Recovery Teams to sift through. The FBI evidence teams ran the rescue efforts and were committed to preserving the dignity of the site and the safety of the rescue workers.

HOPE DENIED

I was not there an hour when I realized that there were not going to be any survivors. The explosion had so pulverized the concrete into dust that there were no pockets of air—only concrete broken down to the size of dirt, sandwiched by broken, concrete beams. Only the media held out hope. They cried out for a rescue, but none could be given, and we all knew it the day following the explosion. Yet we kept digging, and we found bodies. Out of respect to surviving family members, I will not share these moments in detail. It was heart wrenching.

Five of our DEA coworkers were found in the rubble within twenty-five feet of each other. Considering that the DEA office was spread out across nearly the entire ninth floor, one would have thought that they would have been found throughout the blown out core of the broken building. After learning the details of the early morning hours from survivors of the explosion, we were able to understand why so many were found so close together.

Dave Schickendanz, a DEA agent, would surely have been killed that morning had he not walked out of the office as the clock on the wall struck 9:01 am. He was an early riser and had gone to the office early to prepare for a long day. As he walked out of the office, he passed the desk of Carrie Lenz. Gathered around her desk were Carrol Fields, Shelly Bland, Rona Chafey, and Regina Bonny. They were all enjoying the sonogram pictures of Carrie's expected baby.

Regina, a Midwest City Police Corporal who had been working with DEA on a case, walked out and headed to her office down the hall. As Dave got on the elevator, Kenneth McCullough got off and walked toward the front door of the DEA Office. Dave met Alex McCauley, the BATF Resident Agent in Charge of the Oklahoma City Office, as he rode down in the elevator, pushed the button, and the elevator started its descent.

At 9:02 am the bomb exploded, jolting the elevator loose and hurling it downward. Dave and Alex felt the floor of the elevator fall until it came to a crashing stop. The elevator shaft beneath them had filled up with debris from the explosion, just beneath the encapsulated agents, which stopped their rapid descent and spared their lives.

Not understanding what had happened, they pried open the doors and climbed onto the rubble, blinded by the floating, soup-thick concrete dust. After escaping the building through a third floor exit door, Dave and Alex returned in a fruitless effort to find any survivors.

Regina, having just left the DEA office, must surely have crossed paths with Kenneth McCullough as he walked in and passed or maybe even stopped at the desk of Carrie Lenz.

Regina was knocked unconscious by the explosion before she could reach her office. Upon regaining consciousness, she searched desperately for survivors, but a center core of the entire building had collapsed, bringing with it Carrie, Carrol, Shelly, Rona, and Ken.

Regina pulled two injured BATF inspectors from the rubble, one blinded from his injuries and the second pierced by rebar. She guided them through the crumbling walls and floors to the exit and to safety. She returned in a futile effort to find more survivors. Without these firsthand descriptions by Regina and Dave, we would not have known the last moments of our fallen sisters and brothers. Sad as it is, it is the story of life and the destruction of innocence.

MISSED MEMORIAL

On the third day of digging, I got a call from my wife. She reminded me that Billy Graham was slated to speak at the Sunday Memorial Service. Billy Graham was one of my heroes, and my wife did not want me to miss it. However, we had only found four of our DEA friends and were still missing one: Shelly Bland. I did not want to stop till we pulled her from the rubble.

I told her I could not stop. I would at least get some rest when we found Shelly, but not before. I couldn't stop—not even for the Memorial Service and for the once-in-a-lifetime opportunity to hear Billy Graham. I kept digging. On the morning of the fourth day, about the time the Memorial Service had ended, I took a breather at the command post. I stepped outside for a moment when I heard what sounded like the approach of a golf cart near where I stood. I looked up and saw that Billy Graham was being driven to the bombsite on a golf cart! I exclaimed his name out loud, and he turned, looked directly at me, and smiled. The cart proceeded past me and stopped at the entrance to bombsite. I ran up to the cart and watched as Mr. Graham looked over at the devastation. He turned to look at me and reached out to shake my hand. After looking over the wreckage of the federal building, his driver turned the cart around and drove away.

Suddenly, another golf cart pulled up, and there was Mrs. Ruth Graham who sat in the passenger seat. She reached out to me, shook my hand, and thanked me for what I was doing. I told her that it was her who we needed to thank, and after seeing the rubble and paying her respects, they drove away. Had I not missed the Memorial Service, I would have never shaken the hand of the man who shook the world, or looked into the eyes of his steadfast wife who helped to make it all possible. There is a God. On the morning of the fifth day, one of the rescue workers found Shelly.

AWAKE

A lot of us went without sleep for days. I worked on the rocks for five days without sleep. I was a walking dead man. A body can do without water for days. Food, maybe a few months. But sleep? I don't know. I do know what five days without sleep was like for others and me. By the fourth day you run out of adrenaline, and you are just going through the motions of moving debris, without much thought of what is around you. It is like you have tunnel vision and all you can see is the broken, concrete debris in front of you and darkness surrounds it. You reach down to pick it up or move it, but cannot see what is resting beside it. Your actions become mechanical and you do not feel your body as you reach out your arms to remove rubble—you just see your arms enter your vision from the darkness. By the fifth day, you begin to lose your senses. You become a little wacky. Paranoid.

I started to imagine that internal affairs was watching me. For what reason? I don't know. Odd that it was internal affairs that scared me the most. All I knew was that I was losing it and fast.

There was a chain link fence that had been set up to keep the media out, and the portable restrooms were set up outside of that fence. Two US deputy marshals guarded the entrance to keep out anyone who was not involved in the rescue operation.

I climbed down off the rocks and made my way through the gate to the restrooms and encountered the local district attorney standing nearby with John Walsh, of the show "America's Most Wanted." I had been walking with my head hung low when I saw that someone had parked himself in front of me. I looked up and saw the district attorney, a good man. He said he wanted to introduce me to John Walsh. My head was awash with blind spots as I looked at John and shook his hand. His cameraman took a picture of us standing together. Someone handed me a piece of paper to write down my address so they could mail me the picture. I couldn't write. The district attorney took the paper from me, and I told him my address. At least I think I did. I paused, mumbled, and walked on to the portable bathroom.

When I left the restroom, I walked back to the gate in the chain link fence and was stopped by the two US deputy marshals. They said that they had orders to have a couple of DEA agents take me back to the hotel and make me sleep. I was in no position to argue with them and do not even remember the trip to the hotel.

The agents opened my door, and I collapsed on the bed, wide-awake. I guess it was about an hour later I heard some commotion in the hallway and the bang of a fist on my door. I opened the door and found two of my buddies wrestling with another agent. The other agent, Greg, was a good friend of mine. Greg had also been without sleep for days and struggled to go back to the bombsite. We worked together and brought him to his room and tucked him in.

I went back to my room and crashed for five or so hours before I returned to the site. Apparently, all was forgiven and forgotten as the US deputy marshals waved me past, and I went back to work. Somewhere in all this madness was the drive for all of us to honor the slain, pull their bodies from the rubble, and bring them back to their loved ones.

AMERICA REACHES OUT

To say that this act of terror had a monumental impact on the psyche of the American people is an understatement. Americans across the country united in an effort to comfort and support the state of Oklahoma. They expressed their support in truckloads of excavation equipment, boots, gloves, hardhats, shovels, kneepads, biological masks, food, and clothing; they left nothing lacking in the effort to bring out our loved ones from the rubble. America stood with Oklahoma, and it was evident to us all who were able to respond.

I recall walking into a Red Cross support center restroom to wash my hands. When I raised my head, I saw written in lipstick the words "You are looking at a hero...America thanks you." None of us felt like heroes, but these words of support were everywhere. We knew you were with us with every remnant of the building that we removed. It was very emotional for everyone and difficult for all of us to talk about. So we didn't. When I passed other rescue workers in the alleyways and corridors that led from the bombsite, we would pass without words. I could see them hunched down, carrying the same burdens that weighed me down: the work yet to be done, the families depending on us, and perhaps the most heavy burden of all, the senseless and tragic devastation that closed in on us from all sides while we dug through the rocks.

BEHIND THE SCENES

There were also moments of relief that came couched in humor as well as moments of disgust caused by the actions of the media and others.

As we returned from one of the relief centers that had been hastily constructed, we passed by a parking lot that had been walled-off from entry into the vicinity of the bombsite. Members of the media and their broadcasting equipment were contained within this area to prevent visual access to the site. As we walked by it, we observed decals of all of the major networks and many we did not recognize.

One of the newsmen walked to the fence that separated us and asked us if we were actually working in the bombsite. It was a little hard to miss the fact that we were indeed rescue workers, as we were covered in dust from head to toe, wore helmets, had biological masks draped from our necks, and had gloves stuffed in our back pockets. We nodded. He called us over and said he would pay ten thousand dollars to any of us who would give him photos of the victims. I recall that he wore a waist-length leather coat and dressed very nice. His dapper clothing and good looks could not hide the darkness that he had within to make such a request.

We were taken aback by this and shocked by his seeming disregard for the victims and their families. We abruptly walked away as we tried to digest what he had said and the more we walked, the angrier we got. I looked back, and he had disappeared into the maze of motor homes and equipment vans.

That was a first-hand experience of one of the more disappointing moments that we observed while we worked there. Unfortunately, this was only one of many other examples of the cold, calculated methods used by the media to extract information about the bombing.

The last item of note regarding members of the media was the report of a journalist who posed as a fireman and tried to enter the inner sanctum, the rescue site. He was foiled in his attempt and arrested.

Finally, I encountered a disgusting incident that involved a major industrial supply company. In the parking garage beneath one of the buildings were several agencies and companies that provided donated material, support, tools, excavation equipment, clothing, food, and other various items for our assistance.

A few of us had worn out some of our protective gear and headed to the parking garage to replace our gear. As we picked through the excavation equipment at the Red Cross section, we noticed a few hand tools in the adjoining section. Unbeknownst to us, this was the section that belonged to the industrial supply company.

We were told that everything in the garage was donated to the rescue workers to use in the rescue effort, and it was naturally assumed that there were no exceptions. We gathered up a few digging tools when we were confronted by someone who purported to be with the industrial supply company. He told us that we would have to pay for the equipment. We were a little taken aback and asked if he was serious. He was. We walked back to the Red Cross attendant, and she confirmed that they had in fact set up shop and were advertising and selling their wares. Sad.

COMIC RELIEF

The FBI and ATF had their own command posts set up on the road that led into the bombsite. The ATF had a midsized trailer for conventional bomb scene investigations, which they rolled in to use as their command post. They parked it behind and across from the FBI, who had selected the spot closer to the entrance to the perimeter fence that secured the bombsite.

There seemed to be a pecking order lining up, with DEA taking a back seat. The FBI's command post (a large motor home) was tailor-made for the event, larger than the ATF's and prickling with antennas. We, with our usual "fly by the seat of our pants" motto, had no command post.

There has always been a rivalry between the agencies, and it has always been just a lot of fun to the grunts. No one ever means any harm by it, but we take jabs at one another just like opposing teams in a football game. Just a lot of chuckles.

Never to be outdone, as my wife and children will tell you, I went on a classified mission to "acquire" a command post by hopefully persuading some nice person to take pity on us. I brought Bruce Lange with me, a younger agent but nonetheless as skilled in persuasion as me, and headed out.

Bruce and I drove across town to Lee's RV Center, the largest motor home sales lot in Oklahoma City and met with Ron Boyd, the general manager. We told him our dilemma: we planned on being at the site a long time with a large contingent of agents who assisted in the dig, but had nowhere on site for agents to rest. I will never forget his kindness and gentle manner—he was a good man. Ron called the owner, Lee Litchfield.

Without hesitation, they told us to go pick out the largest, nicest motor home on the lot and take off. We did just that. Lee and Ron gave from the heart. What a couple of stand up Americans. Before we headed back to the site, we stopped at a sign company and had them make a sign which identified the beast as the DEA command post and set it aside.

We drove back to downtown Oklahoma City and maneuvered the beast down the twisting roads leading up to the bombsite. We eyed around for a spot and determined that if we were careful, we could just barely squeeze in between the FBI command post and the chain link fence perimeter.

As we rolled past the ATF and FBI command posts, we looked over at the ATF to see their eyes pop out of their sockets as they took in the size of our motor home. They looked inside, watching me place the DEA command post sign in the window and started laughing, knowing full well what we were about to do. Bruce hopped out and directed me into the very tight space that separated the FBI from the bombsite. I was not even sure it would fit, but I pushed that beast to its limits. I was going to shove it in there if I had to pry it in with my bare hands, and I nearly had to do just that.

The Fan Belt Inspectors were not happy and stared me down as I squeezed that puppy in there and cranked up the satellite dish and outside awning. Looking back, I now realize how immature and petty I was, even a little too childish. Whatever. But God has a way of making you pay for those adolescent deeds. My son was recently hired as a Special Agent for the FBI. Oh bother.

FAREWELL AND GODSPEED

I left Oklahoma City on the tenth day when they pulled all the rescue workers off the rocks and brought in the heavy machinery. I will never forget our friends we lost, the children, mothers, fathers, grandmothers, grandfathers, sons, and daughters—Americans all.

It was a long and somber drive home, alone.

Tim standing by his patrol car
in El Paso, Texas in 1974.

Tim standing on the tarmac at Bagram Air Base, preparing
for a mission. The Hindu Kush Mountains in northern
Afghanistan lie in the background.

Tim with fellow agents and task force officers at the bombsite in Oklahoma City, Oklahoma in April 1995.

Tim and Bruce Lange presenting Ron Boyd (center) with the DEA Command Center sign in appreciation for his providing us a mobile command center at the Oklahoma City bombing.

The bomber, Abdul Shaheed, walking past the surveillance vehicle just before Tim tackled him attempting to board the bus in the background. Shaheed is carrying the sack containing the bomb.

Tim is standing at the bomber arrest scene, immediately following the arrest of the suicide bomber.

Tim and Jeff apprehending Shaheed, as taken by the Dutch Special Forces Apache helicopter that hovered above to hold back the crowd.

A close up of the arrest. Tim holds the bomber in a headlock while Jeff secures his right side to prevent him from setting off the IED with the detonator in his vest.

Abdul Shaheed, the bomber, had already killed the five Afghan security agents when Tim and Jeff arrested him. He was en route to attack an American base in Kabul on April 21, 2004.

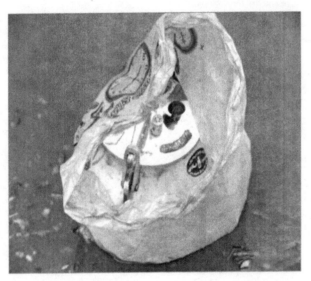

The bomb, an Iranian pressure cooker, was fused and loaded with over three kilograms (six and a half pounds) of high explosives and projectiles.

The US Attorney General, Alberto Gonzales, DEA Administrator Karen Tandy, and the Acting Attorney General, Robert McCallum, present Tim Sellers and Jeff Higgins with the Award for Exceptional Heroism at Constitutional Hall in Washington, DC on August 31, 2005.

CHAPTER FIVE

GUNSLINGERS

WHO YOU GONNA CALL?

There is a song in "Ghostbusters" which goes something like: "If there's something strange in your neighborhood, who ya gonna call? Ghostbusters!"

This rings true of the desperation one must feel when confronted with an enemy who is free to attack anywhere, anytime, and anyone—without warning. You have got to be desperate when the only one left to call is someone with a handle like that! When someone with the capability threatens to kill a DEA agent and there is no specific target, time, or location, who are you going to call? Well, we didn't know whom to call either, so we just answered the call ourselves.

The threat came from four thugs who discussed offing a DEA agent. A call was made, and the order was given. "Find someone to kill him...he's an agent...yeah, DEA." That was all that was said, but it was enough. Unbeknownst to them, US Customs (a predecessor component of US Homeland Security) had a wire up on their phone, and they had paid attention.

The thugs, three of Mexican nationality and one an American by the name of Luis Alvarado, were members of a Mexican drug cartel known as the Juarez Cartel. The Juarez Cartel was the dominant drug cartel in Mexico during the late 1980s to early 1990s, continuing into the late 1990s as a formidable cartel. Luis was the supplier of stolen vehicles for a segment of the Mexican Federal Judicial Police (the Federales) in Juarez who were closely associated with the Juarez Cartel. He traded vehicles in exchange for their protection for years and was well known to the El Paso Police Department. It was rumored that Luis also moved tons of marijuana and hundreds of kilos of cocaine through the waters that separated Mexico and the United States. One of the thugs with Luis was a Juarez cop, and it was he who ordered the hit.

It didn't take long after hearing the order to kill a DEA agent on the wiretap for US Customs Special Agent Tom Morgan to burn up the phone line to the El Paso Field Division, where I was assigned. Tom was a customs pilot, sharp-looking, and a black belt in karate. (Why didn't he make movies?) Tom said he was going to come over and told us to get the coffee pot on. Telling us that the meeting required coffee told us all we needed to know: it was going to be a long and interesting night. El Paso Police Detective Sal Olivarez and I started the coffee pot and sat down to wait for Tom's arrival. As we sat, we swapped some war stories, some of them involving the both of us. Sal and I had partnered up a while back and had really hit it off. He was a kindly person, with a pit bull's determination to catch bad guys. He was also a top-notch gumshoe. He knew his job and had contacts everywhere. With Sal involved, I knew that we wouldn't let Tom down.

Tom came up to our office and after a short meet and greet, laid out the situation to the two of us. A background check on Luis proved that he was in fact closely associated with the Juarez Police. Further, he was heavily involved in supplying them stolen vehicles and had a violent arrest record. Luis and a few of his buddies were recently arrested by the El Paso Police Department for theft of auto. For some reason, they thought that an undercover DEA agent was responsible for their arrests. Sal and I checked around the office with the other agents to determine who might be involved in the arrest of these bad boys in the auto theft ring, and no one knew anything about it.

How come every bad guy who has a bad day and gets put in jail has to blame it on us? Do they ever think that maybe it could have been something they did? Do they consider that maybe they were just unlucky or just a little sloppy? No. That would make it their fault. These toads want to kill one of us because some meatball doesn't want to man up and accept responsibility for his bad luck.

One of those arrested with Luis was the son of a popular communist in Juarez and led a major auto theft ring over there. Luis had boasted that he had supplied over a thousand cars a year to the Mexican Federales and drug traffickers. This was probably a major overstatement, but he was nonetheless a player and a major one at that. One of their cohorts was recently arrested with a large weapons cache, and word was on the streets that Luis was trying to score more weapons to replace the weapons that had been seized.

Now we had a perplexing dilemma. Did they, in fact, want to kill a DEA agent or was it someone they *thought* was a DEA agent, like a cop or agent from a different federal agency? A lot of crooks refer to any cop working drugs as a DEA agent. But there are local cops, state cops, FBI, Homeland Security, and a lot of other agencies that work drugs. There are a limited number of DEA agents, and it is common to blame us rather than the agency that actually conducted the investigation. We could not confirm that DEA had anything to do with their arrests, so there may have been a misunderstanding in play. If we did not correctly identify the target, we could not warn them of the danger. The bad guys obviously had the capability and the motive to kill the target, but who? When? We concluded that we had to work on the premise that these guys were determined to kill a DEA agent, as we could not prove otherwise. To ignore the threat could have tragic consequences.

ROPE A DOPE

Luckily, Tom did not come into our office empty-handed. He had a snitch that could possibly provide some help. Tom called him up and told him to come down to the office. When he arrived, we brought him into the briefing room and determined that he was solid. The snitch was close to one of Luis Avarado's dirtball buddies and could make an introduction of an undercover agent.

After we dumped the snitch, we parlayed on a strategy to stop the threat. We would have to penetrate this group and ferret out the identity of the agent they had plotted to kill without being exposed. If they got wind of any operation, they would pull up stakes and go into stealth mode, leaving us without the ability to stop the hit.

Our options were limited. Picking up Luis with no leverage would be weak. He was a seasoned crook, so he would know we had nothing and just tell us to pound sand. We had to get leverage. We had to catch him dirty. We needed to go undercover and reach into this organization to squeeze it for an opportunity to facilitate their desire to break the law. We would then hammer down on them and find out the identity of their target.

Luis had already indicated a desire to buy weapons and move a lot of cocaine. The snitch had corroborated this. We decided that one of us needed to approach Luis in an undercover role as a weapons trafficker and offer weapons for dope. If we could catch him dirty we might be able to roll him (make him talk). If we could pressure him to give up the identity of the DEA agent he wanted to kill, we could stop the threat, or at a minimum, protect the agent. I volunteered to do the deed. Why not? It looked like a lot of fun.

We ordered the snitch to arrange a meeting with Luis through his buddy. The snitch contacted Luis' buddy and told him that he knew someone who is in the weapons business and moves a lot of dope. This "someone" was in short supply of dope and needed a hook up. The dirtball's interest was piqued. He said that he would arrange a meet between Luis and the snitch's "someone." I was, of course, that "someone," and Luis and I were about to go on our first date.

Before I could do anything, I had to do one thing first—paperwork, and lots of it. Paper, paper, paper. You have no idea how much paper you have to write for this kind of operation, not to mention all the permission slips you have to get to walk out the door and meet with someone who wanted to kill a DEA agent. What a bother.

BLARNEY FOR THE STONED

I walked into an Italian food restaurant in central El Paso and grabbed the back table with my back to the wall. This is instinct for any cop, or any real crook. I got there first. Nearby sat a few undercover cops who were there to keep a watchful eye on me. I was never out of the sight of my partner Sal, who watched over me like a guardian angel.

Tom oversaw the outside surveillance and made sure they spotted Luis when he drove up. The outside agents and cops watched the comings and goings of all the patrons. They were well-placed to follow Luis after the meet. It's always tough on the outside guys. They have to stay alert during the many hours of boredom while they watch for the target. They are under a lot of pressure not to miss the crook when he drives up or when he drives away. The inside guys get to chow down on the G's dime.

We were all set up when the outside surveillance called the inside boys and said that Luis had just arrived alone and parked in the rear. They gave me the heads up. As Luis walked into the restaurant, he scanned the room. I nodded to him as he walked over and sat down. He looked a little slick —not someone you would want your daughter to bring home. He also looked a little stoned. His eyes were glassy, and he reeked of marijuana.

"Hey, Luis. Sit down. Thanks for coming."

"You a real cowboy?"

"Nope. I only dress this way when I sing for the Village People. Order up—the lasagna is good."

We danced around a little with the small talk—a little blarney for the stoned, if you will—and then got down to business. Luis broke the ice.

"Look, my people in Mexico are sicarios (hit men). They work for the Federales. They need guns. A lot of guns. They have been running into a lot of problems lately, and they need to protect their loads."

"Luis, I'm good with that. I need some powder (cocaine) and lots of it, but I don't need trouble on both sides of the border. It's hard enough working over here, but doing deals for weapons with cops in Mexico is risky. I don't need the grief." It was like a match made in heaven, but I wanted him to beg.

"Hey, man, you will be dealing only with me. They don't want to meet anyone. I will be the front man."

"Okay, but I don't want them showing up. I don't care how cool they are. I don't know these dudes, and I don't want to meet them." And pigs fly. Of course I wanted to meet them.

"No problem. Just let me handle it, and I'll take care of it."

Now all I had to do was massage his brain a little and make him love me. I laid down a scam that I had an army surplus store near Ft. Bliss and that lots of soldiers streamed in and out with gear for hard cash. I convinced him that I had made a few alliances with soldiers I trusted who would bring in weapons from the field and unload them on me.

"All they ask is that I don't sell the guns in the US. They want me to keep them for my private collection, because they don't want the guns coming back to haunt them."

"Sounds good. I want ten M-16 machineguns, hand grenades, and sixteen shoulder-fired LAWS (Light Anti-Tank Weapons Systems) rockets. How soon can I get them?"

"Ease up there, Luis. This is a two way street. I want powder."

"I can swap for dope, but I want to buy first before I hook you up."

Luis was enthralled. He had hit the jackpot. His eyeballs rolled in his head, and I'm sure all he could see were dollar signs.

I continued to weave the tapestry of deception with the ease of a brain surgeon. I gently wooed him into a state of hypnotic trance as I led him down the path to his destruction. Oh, what a great job I had! He was so blinded by his greed that he didn't realize that an old cowboy like me was jerking his chain. I'm still amazed that they actually paid me to have this much fun. He was putty in my hands. Oh, silly man.

It was his idea to get his hands on a load of weapons from the start...all I did was convince him that I was the candy man. He agreed to swap the weapons for dope but insisted that they buy the weapons first and see how that goes. He said that his people could do a couple hundred kilos of coke a month. He offered me seventy-five pounds of marijuana with more later, but he had to clear it with his people first.

We went back and forth a while and finally agreed to meet after he met with his contacts and worked out the details. As we walked out together, he eyed my red Corvette and smiled.

"Don't even think about it, Luis."

We parted as friends, or so he thought. The surveillance team hitched up to his rear and followed him all the way to the east side and put him to bed.

We returned to the office and contacted the military to arrange for the weapons to be used in the operation. I called my old friend, Vic "Polygraph" Maldonado with the Bureau of Alcohol, Tobacco, and Firearms. If we did sell them weapons for export to Mexico, it would be a violation of the Neutrality Act, and we wanted BATF in on it. Vic's responsibility was to facilitate the delivery of the weapons with the military while I continued meetings and phone calls with Luis. Luis was probably meeting with his people throughout the next several days, while we did the same. Just like us, he pulled out all the stops to make this deal happen. He just didn't know that we were working for different results.

FRANK IS A HANDYMAN

During one of my meetings with Luis, he said that Frank Herrera was the lead enforcer for this group of toads. Recently, Frank had executed a couple of guys he thought had snitched. I think Luis wanted to get the point across that I had better not be a cop or there were going to be consequences. He proceeded to describe how effective an enforcer Frank really was. Frank drove the first victim to the desert outside of Juarez and forced him to dig a hole and stand in it. Frank stuck a gun to his head, pulled the trigger, and killed him. Frank kicked a little dirt on him and left.

Frank executed a second poor soul soon thereafter. He took this one out to the desert near where the last one was buried and also made him dig a hole. Frank poured gasoline on him and then lit him up. He never bothered to bury him. He was still smoking when Frank drove off.

There was a third. Luis went to Juarez to see Frank to talk about his deal with me. Luis walked into a safe house, which was lost in an old ramshackle neighborhood near the outskirts of town. As he walked through the house, Luis saw something that hung from the exposed rafters. He realized that it was a man. Luis said he was taken aback and scurried past him to a room in back of the house where Frank waited for him.

Frank was nonchalant about what Luis said he saw only to mention that this is what they did to snitches. Frank had taken a break from torturing the snitch with a pair of pliers. As Frank discussed the deal for the weapons and cocaine, he complained that his hands ached from his "little project." Luis told me that Frank said he wanted to take a hard look at me—close up—before he made any decisions. I didn't think he meant well by that statement, and I got the willies just hearing it.

I was a little surprised that Luis would share so much with me. Apparently, he was under my spell, but he had to make sure that he was right about me. If he set this deal up with a cop, Luis was a dead man. It was Luis who would hang from the rafters right alongside of me. Frank was the man, and I would have to get past him to make this deal happen. I was stirring up a hornet's nest, and I realized that the deeper I got into this deal, the less chance I had of not getting stung.

During one of our telephone conversations, Luis told me that he was at home and couldn't talk with his girlfriend and kids there, so he talked to me in code. He responded to my questions with yes or no for the most part. But the longer we talked, the more open he became, as if unconcerned about who listened.

"My people want to do the deal with you in Mexico, not here. Deliver the weapons there, and we'll give you what you want."

"What are you smoking? The closest I will ever get to Mexico is a drive-thru at Taco Bell." Could this be a trap? Hmmm. Gee. Gosh. I don't know; they seemed like such nice people.

"Don't worry so much. They just want to meet you. The Federales will protect you." Yeah, that's like the coyote guarding the chicken house. Cluck, cluck. I started shoveling fast—if I didn't, it would be them shoveling dirt on me.

"You said they didn't want to meet anyone. What changed?"

"They want to work things out face to face. They want more guns later and want to grease this deal. Make sure it goes smoothly."

"I'm not going to step foot in Mexico with any weapons. It's just not going to happen. If they want to do this deal, they need to shag their behinds over the bridge or tread water, because I'm not going to step foot on their turf."

He finally let go of the Mexico thing. But Luis insisted that the Federales would not do the deal unless I went through Frank. "All you need to do is meet Frank and let him see you're for real. If Frank gives the deal the green light, the Feds will follow through."

Wait a minute. Frank? Did he say Frank? That nice man who carries around pliers in his back pocket?

"Are you serious?! After everything you've told me about Frank, do you really expect me to meet him in person? I'm not going to meet the tool man, so knock it off."

My mouth was saying no, but inside I was dying to meet this monster. I was intrigued.

Even though Luis assured me that the Federales controlled Frank and I had nothing to worry about, I wondered what kind of a dark soul would torture a living man and watch him slowly die? Frank was one of those kinds of men. Evil was like heroin in his veins. "Hard as he tried, he would never make his soul as dark as he wanted it." It was clear after my conversation with Luis that if I didn't meet Frank, there would be no deal. That was it.

I guess I was a little loco, because I decided a meeting with Frank was worth the risk. Everyone involved in my deal was concerned about this man I had to meet. We did a background on Frank and found out that he was a US citizen on probation with a long track record with the law. Our sources confirmed the stories of Frank's murderous rampages. He had been closely associated with the Juarez Cartel for many years, and they relied upon him to shed a little light on the hidden motives and actions of those they suspected of snitching or skimming loads of dope and cash.

This didn't change my decision to meet Frank. It was just another day on the job to me, and this only pumped the adrenaline a little more. Isn't that why all of us agents get into this line of work anyway? I mean, I could have been an astronaut. I considered it real hard, but finally concluded that my fear of heights (and math) would be a detriment. So I settled on becoming a DEA agent. In my mind, it was safer.

ALMOST WON A VACATION TO MEXICO

Frank wanted to meet Luis and me at an upscale restaurant on Interstate 10. We were to discuss the proposed meeting with the main players and lay down the game plan. Luis emphasized that it was up to Frank to determine if I was legit.

We gathered up the forces on the day of the meet and made an operational plan that involved Customs, BATF, the El Paso Police

Department, and DEA. While we made the final arrangements, a wrench was thrown into the works. The snitch called Tom and said that he found out that Frank and his goons were going to kidnap me and take me to Mexico if Frank was not convinced I was legit. Or even worse, that I was a cop.

That stepped up the commotion and a lot of calls had to be made for approvals to allow me to walk into a possible ambush. We dropped back and retrofitted the ops (operational) plan to include a sniper team on the roof of the strip mall that surrounded the restaurant and a load of surveillance and tactical teams to prevent my kidnapping and arrest the defendants if things blew up. Everyone headed out to set up.

The outside surveillance called and said that Luis was outside with three guys, two on foot and two in a tan pickup truck. It was no surprise that they had lied when they said that it would be just Frank, Luis, and myself at the restaurant. They just couldn't help it. They were liars.

The surveillance team called again and said that they had observed the guys in the tan pickup meet with some dudes in a Mercury Marquis with darkened windows (the vehicle of choice for the Federales) that was parked in the lot adjacent to the restaurant. They identified one more vehicle in the lot and concluded that the kidnapping was probably a happening deal if I failed. I fired up the Corvette and headed to the restaurant. Sal, ever the mother, kept a watchful eye on me from his vehicle as he followed me in. I had hoped to catch the four guys standing outside to throw them off their game.

As I drove up into the lot, I saw two guys I had not seen before who stood outside with Luis. I recognized Frank from his photo, and the second I assumed was one of the main players. They glanced up at me as I pulled up to them and ejected out of my Corvette.

In a raised voice, I scolded Luis, "I told you that you weren't supposed to have anyone else here! Who are these guys?!" The third guy quickly walked to the passenger side of the truck, and a fourth guy who sat in the truck backed it out of the parking place and headed out to the parking lot exit.

I looked at Frank and said I was not happy, but reached out my hand and offered it. He was stunned at my reaction but made the best of it and reciprocated, shaking my hand. I looked at Luis and motioned for him to follow us as we walked into the restaurant. Frank was a hard man. I had to deal with him straight up. No messing around. He had that look of death in his eyes and a no-nonsense demeanor.

I could not help but look at his hands when he talked. I couldn't stop thinking about the men he had killed. It was difficult to break bread with this low life, but I had to win him over. We had no hope of finding out the identity of their target unless I succeeded. I knew that if I failed, they would be unable to take me alive to Juarez, as our tactical units would prevent that from happening. But there were no guarantees that Dr. Evil (Frank) was not determined to at least take me out if things went south.

Things were tense during the first thirty minutes of conversation. We were like a couple of bulls butting heads. If I didn't break through soon, we were not going to make it. I figured at this point, I had nothing to lose.

I started to rattle off some humdinger zingers designed to make them giggle like little girls. I used an old one that I had told many times in the past. I told Frank about the time that I went to the movies a few years back: "Here I was all sprawled out across three seats, when the usher walked up to me and said, 'Sorry, sir, but you're only allowed one seat.' I just looked up at him and groaned, but didn't budge. The usher became impatient, 'Sir, if you don't get up from there, I'm going to have to call the manager.' I just kept groaning—heck, that's all I could get out. The manager returned with the usher and together they couldn't get me to budge. Finally, they called the cops. A cop arrived, took a hard look at the situation, and belted out, 'Okay cowboy, what's your name?' 'Tim,' I moaned. 'Where ya from, Tim?' With pain in my voice, I replied, 'The balcony.'"

Frank bellowed out in laughter and knocked over his water glass, spilling water everywhere. My joke went a long way in breaking the ice, and the more I threw at him, the more he chuckled. By golly it worked. Frank was like putty in my hands. Before long, we were best friends—you know, the class bully and the class clown. It is amazing what a little laughter will do to ease tensions and mend fences.

Frank bought into it, and he agreed to let me meet the main players to make the deal. I told him I would make the arrangements through Luis to show them the weapons. Frank also refused to swap the weapons for dope, but was sure his people would pay cash. I knew this was the hammer we hoped to find. The guns were enough of a violation to use as leverage to find out their intended target of assassination, so I did not press the matter. I had their assurances that if the weapons deal went well, I could get a boatload of cocaine. At this point, it was not the cocaine on my mind, but the leverage the gun deal would give us to save the agent they wanted to kill. Now my only problem was figuring out how I was going get to my Corvette without taking an unscheduled vacation to Mexico.

We got up to leave, and I walked with them to the exit. I figured that if I failed to convince Frank, the snatch would take place in the parking lot as I walked to the vehicle. I had to delay going out till I heard from the outside boys that it was all clear. As we approached the door, I told Frank I had to make a pit stop and would see him later. I said my goodbyes, turned around, and headed to the men's room. He smiled and left with Luis. After I washed my hands about ten times, I got bored as I waited for them to leave and restocked the toilet paper and soap bars. One of the inside surveillance boys walked in and stood there staring at me. He watched as I wiped down the counter and asked, "Sellers. What the heck are you doing? It's all clear. They all loaded up and left." Frank and Luis were followed out of the parking lot by the darkened Mercury Marquis and the tan pick up. I guess I had convinced Frank. Whew.

THE WEAPONS FLASH

The next day, I called Luis and said the weapons were in and I was ready to show the main dude what we had. He arranged a meet at a restaurant located in a central El Paso shopping mall the following day. I called Vic with BATF, and he rounded up a few of the weapons: an M-16, an inert grenade, and one inert LAWS rocket. The plan was to meet Luis and the chief crook in charge in the restaurant, walk out with him to the parking lot, and enter a blue panel van. Vic would be inside the van to demo the weapons.

The following day, I met with the bad guys at the restaurant. We wasted no time walking out to the parking lot and rapped on the door of the van that held Vic and the weapons. We all bent over and climbed inside. Vic dazzled them with his boyish smile and obvious mechanical skills as he walked them through the operation of the M-16 and one LAWS rocket. He also pulled out the one inert hand grenade, which really wowed them. What is it with these dudes? They all look like agents—you know, all-American, handsome, dimples, winning smiles—heck, I saw right away that Vic was a Fed. If you picked out a guy for a role as a Fed in a movie, it would be

Vic. Anyway, I might have been able to pick out Vic, but the bad dudes apparently didn't. Maybe it is because I read the script.

After that, it was a deal. I would meet the main targets at a local burger joint near the corner of Dyer and Fred Wilson. Prior to meeting with them, our surveillance teams would locate the missing players (Luis and Dr. Evil) and arrest them when the deal was done. We wired up a house in a nearby neighborhood and loaded the garage with cameras. The plan was to meet them, see the money, have them follow me to the house, open the garage door, and have them drive in. Inside, Vic and I would show them the weapons. When they paid us the cash, we would load the weapons into the back of their truck and then give the bust signal.

The following day, I met three of the main players at the local burger joint. While we parlayed, one of them boasted that he was a cop from Juarez. The main dude lifted up a white cloth sack and opened it up, displaying eighteen thousand dollars. He had brought a little extra in case there was a hitch. We drove to the house, opened the garage, and drove in. We had fifty-four M-67 hand grenades, ten M-16 machineguns, and sixteen M72A2 LAWS rockets. Vic did his magic, and then we loaded up the weapons into the back of their truck. We gave the bust signal, and the raid team scrambled through the inside garage door and slammed the two crooks to the ground. We made calls to the other teams who had the missing links under surveillance and ordered them picked up. It went down without a hitch.

Now all we had to do was make one of them give up the goods on the plot to kill the agent. We dragged Luis into the holding cell at the DEA office, and we worked him hard. After twenty minutes, he was ready to deal. He gave up the goose. The target of the hit was not a DEA agent but an El Paso Police Detective who had arrested Luis' buddies and really choked off the auto theft ring that supplied cars to the Federales. That is all we cared about. We immediately called the police department and got the detective on the phone to give him a heads up. With a lot more work on Luis and some of the other defendants, we determined the threat had passed and the cop could sleep soundly at night. Any thoughts they may have had about whacking that cop ended in the aftermath of their arrests. What began as an investigation into the hit on a DEA agent led us to the identity of the real target, so we could stop any threat to his life, and allowed us to hammer the crooks to boot. All the bad guys plead guilty and served time for violations of the Neutrality Act for trying to export weapons to Mexico. But to put the icing on the cake, I'd gotten through it with my hide still intact. I'd call that a successful mission.

CHAPTER SIX

RODE HARD

A POCKET FULL OF DIMES

I had pretty much decided I was at the end of my career as a DEA agent. I thought things were winding down, and I thought about getting myself a rocking chair or a fishing pole. Looking around, I saw a lot of young, strong, and dang-it-all, handsome agents rushing around the office, in and out, talking about wiretaps, cell phones, and intergalactic surveillances. The old ways, working undercover, working snitches, were of days gone by. The new technological advances, such as computers, wiretaps, and blackberries changed the daily routine of the street agent. The younger DEA agents did not forget the old ways; they just never knew them. I really did not follow all of the changes going on in DEA and knew that these young studs had outclassed me. I had just started to learn how to open my emails on the government computers. They, on the other hand, were rippin' up the Internet to search the financial records of major traffickers without ever leaving their desks.

I remember years ago, we had to carry a pocket full of dimes around for the pay phone. We would dial those numbers from a pay phone while working undercover to patch together some kind of drug deal. Then one day I got my hands on the office mobile phone. It was called a mobile phone, but what they really meant was you could carry it to the car and drive it around. It was as big as a lunchbox and would pull your arm out of its socket if you walked around with it. I really thought I was pretty cool with that phone. Nobody ever called me on it. But that was as high tech as I ever got.

I never wore an earring, but did let my hair down (before it all went away). I had driven fast cars, wore five hundred dollar cowboy hats, and five hundred dollar boots. Northern agents called us border rats, and border rats we were. I don't think it was meant to be a compliment. But the handle stuck, and we embraced it. We were comfortably sandwiched between two countries—immersed in the Spanish culture yet Texan to the core. Looking back, I guess we would best be described as "cocaine cowboys" when we worked undercover. This was a term coined in the 2006 documentary entitled *Cocaine Cowboys* which chronicled the transformation of Miami into the cocaine capitol of the world by the "cocaine cowboys" of the South American drug cartels. The name suited us a lot better, as we blended with the Wild West world of Mexican drug traffickers along the border.

The bad guys dressed like cowboys and looked pretty darned good. In the beginning, I figured that if I was going to fit in, I would have to spend a little more money on a nice Stetson and ostrich boots, so I could can the sweaty straw. So off I went to the local cowboy store and bought myself some new duds. I hid it from my wife—for about two hours. When I left to go to work that night, she picked right up on it and asked me what the heck was on my head. I asked her what she was talking about, figuring I was in stealth mode, and she pointed right up to the top of my head and said, "That."

Not to be one to step back from a good fight, but knowing I might not survive the first round of fire, I gave it up (I was hoping she would not notice the boots, and if I took the hit for the hat, I could get out before there was too much collateral damage). Man, did I shortchange the little lady. She snapped on the boots before I could do penance on the hat. She went on to tell me about the three little kids we had, and how we had a hard enough time making ends meet. A quick confession, one, maybe two calls for forgiveness, and I might make it out the door. No deal. I took it like a man. And then when I picked myself up off the floor, I made a mad dash to the door, dipping and dodging as I outran the little woman. To this day, I won't come home with a new pair of boots without clearing it with the war department first.

Back to being a super cocaine cowboy. Cocaine cowboys (undercover border rats) knew how to buy dope. We wanted it all: small pieces of heroin, wheelbarrows full of cocaine, and truckloads of marijuana. We were never any good with the paperwork, but we could talk a fast game and hit a homerun once in a while. We spent most of our time hiding from management and taking shortcuts to get away from the ever-multiplying rules of a large government bureaucracy.

Because of people like me, they changed all the rules. I could live with that, but throw in a computer and other high tech investigative methods, and my playing field got pretty small. Border rats just did not know how to operate in this new world. We liked the feel of dope on the table. The thrill of slamming some mope on the floor as we crashed into his home at two-dark-thirty looking for guns and dope.

Most of us border rats had already retired and moved on to other things, but I kind of held on, milking Uncle Sugar for the last few drops of that little green paycheck that I got every two weeks. Come to think of it, they stopped mailing me my paycheck and deposited it directly into my account years back. I never did like that deal. Kind of felt like I was being robbed. Anyhow, I figured that Uncle was on to me and felt like I was told to move into the 21st century, or move out to the pasture with the rest of the old bulls.

PUPPY IN THE ROUND CAN

In the spring of 2004, DEA asked for volunteers to work in Afghanistan to establish a presence there. There was a lot a buzz around the office about who would put in for the job. As they went through the names of those in the office qualified to do it, they discounted me immediately. I was probably the oldest agent in our division. It was apparent they believed I was past my prime, walking around the office as I waited for the grim reaper to make a pick up.

Younger agents felt strongly that they were better suited for this dangerous assignment to Afghanistan. One in particular, a young agent and a law school graduate with five years on the job, commented to me that the streets were too tough for old agents, and that they had no business working enforcement anymore. He said that older agents lost their ability to react or perform tactically and would put other agents' lives in jeopardy. Was he right? Was this bold life all over for me or could Afghanistan be a great last hurrah? What was the need to put myself in the line of fire again? Oh, what the heck, I threw my hat in the ring. I figured all my kids were grown up, and my wife always stood with me through thick and thin. Besides, I never got anything I put in for before, so what were the odds?

Months passed. I did not hear anything and gave up—again. I tossed around in my mind thoughts of retirement. I put some numbers together and figured I could make it on my pension if I got a job at Walmart as a greeter. But I had this gnawing thought in the back of my head. I had a really hard time believing that it was all over. What about Afghanistan? It was probably the only place no one wanted to go. How much competition could there be for that job? I scoffed at myself because I knew that it was a young man's game and HQ wasn't going to call. I hoped there was more but knew it was time. It was over, and I gave up. I went to the office and filled out the form for retirement. I set it in the fax machine.

The phone rang. It was Raul Morales, an old friend in headquarters, one of the few left from the old days. Raul asked me how I was, and we chitchatted. Deep in the recesses of my fat head, I vaguely recalled that Raul was on the foreign desk. These guys decide which agents go to what countries.

Knowing I had put in for over 290 foreign jobs and never, no never, got one, I gasped. While Raul jabbered about the good ol' days, I let myself imagine exotic locations like Milan, Paris, Costa Rica, hoping beyond hope that this was the call. My ship was coming in. A foreign deal. Far away places. Finally!

Raul rattled away on the other end about how bad he had it. I could not take it anymore and interrupted him. I jerked the words out from my mouth and asked him if he was on the foreign desk. He said yes. I knew he had something on his mind and allowed the conversation to pause. Then he started crying about working in headquarters again.

I interrupted him. I asked him what section he was in. Man, I wanted it to be Europe or Central America real bad. I asked, "Europe?" Nope. "Central America?" Nope. He said he worked the Central Asia Desk. I said with a little lift in my voice, "Thailand?"

"Nope. That's East Asia, bud. You wish," Raul snorted. He said he pulled my name from a long list of names wanting overseas jobs. My heart skipped a beat as I wondered, where in the heck is Central Asia? Haltingly, he asked, "How 'bout…Afghanistan?" It was as if he was afraid of my reaction. (Our mutual friend Tina Hinojos had called Raul and pointed out that I had put in for Afghanistan, hoping that Raul would "help" me get selected. What an angel.)

Well, you don't get these calls but once in your career, and you better not look a gift horse in the mouth. Who knows, I thought, maybe I could get some cool souvenirs over there.

Without hesitation, I said I'd take it, acting as if I accepted assignments like this all the time. He said he would put me in touch with the Afghanistan desk to give me the details. There were no details. DEA had not been there since 1976, and I was going to be one of the first agents over there to help build an office. While I thanked him, I dug out my world atlas and tried to figure out where in the heck Afghanistan was. I hung up, took a deep breath, and called the war department. While I punched the numbers on the phone, I pulled the request to retire out of the fax machine and popped that puppy in the round can.

I had already sold my wife on the idea of retiring, and she looked forward to it. She asked me if Afghanistan was what I wanted. When I look back, I realize that my wife has been the ultimate trooper throughout my career. She packed up, moved, hid out from bad guys, cooked breakfast for fifteen undercover agents camped out in her living room as they held surveillance over a neighboring house, raised three small kids, and did it all without a lot of money. She never complained. Never once told me no. I respected and loved her for her quiet, tender, steadfast support. She has and will always have veto power. I told her it would be a great adventure. She told me to go for it. I never doubted.

AIR RUSSIA

I had two weeks to get there. Got my shots, got my gear, said goodbye, and flew off to Washington DC. Wait a second. Did I say gear? What gear? I asked them what to bring, and HQ said, "Don't worry about getting anything before you come. Just bring your raid gear, and we'll send you some 'stuff' when you get to Afghanistan." I did not like the sound of that. DEA stands for "Don't Expect Anything," and this was not my first rodeo. I knew that if I depended on them to send me gear, I would come up short. The raid gear they told me to bring along was designed for street work in the US, but wouldn't stop a Taliban bullet. I bugged DEA to cough up some dough so I could buy some tactical stuff. HQ gave me a $200 dollar limit and said, "Go shopping at Wal-Mart, but remember to save your receipts."

Now, I knew there was a nearby processing station at Ft. Bliss (in El Paso) for anyone going over to the sand box and even asked if I could swing by there and pick up some of that "stuff" they talked about. This would have required a little effort on DEA's part to make a few calls, but that was too much to ask for. The Feebs (FBI) had all the high-speed gear the military could offer. They all flew into Ft. Bliss, three blocks from my house, and got their "stuff" at this processing station. All I would have had to do was drive ten minutes, back up my truck, and load 'em up. But DEA wouldn't make the calls. Oh well. I knew I fought a losing battle, so I manned up, bought $200 worth of Slim Jims and popcorn at Walmart, and headed off to DC.

It was there at the Washington Dulles Airport concourse that I met up with Frank Thompson, a younger agent with a family. I told him to look for an old guy with no hair on his head sporting a white goatee. He spotted me in the crowd as I walked toward the gate. I carried a backpack stuffed with my gear (snacks). He said I kind of stood out. I laughed and wondered to myself what he meant. Without prompting, he laughed along with me and said that I was definitely an old fart and the oldest agent he had ever seen. Then he asked me what I was thinking. He meant, what in the heck is a fifty-two year old man thinking, volunteering to go a war zone?

He laughed again and still tells the story of how he spotted me in the crowd—a real geezer. We traveled together in business class, stopping in London for a change of flights and a shower. I had never traveled business class before. The flight over was a bit extravagant for an old cowboy from Texas. There is a rule for government travelers that if their trip is longer than fifteen hours, the traveler can go business class. In business class, the seats lay flat with individual movie screens, dinner, and all of the perks available to first class travelers. I leaned back in my seat, stretched my legs out, and parked my boots on the leather foot extension, while I thought to myself, "I'm a long way from Texas!" I guzzled down a bottle of beer, pulled my lid down over my eyes, and nodded off, grinning from ear to ear. Onward to Islamabad, and so it began.

We arrived in Islamabad, Pakistan to await the United Nations flight into Kabul. We exited the plane at the airport in Islamabad and stood in a long line of incoming passengers who awaited clearance by Pakistani customs. I could see Rick from the Dallas DEA office, an old friend of mine, in the distance waiting for us. He had been in Pakistan for a few years and was there to pick us up and bring us to a hotel for a night. When the line got up to the front, I was asked for my passport and DEA credentials by some toothy guy who wore something that I think was supposed to be a uniform. He studied my papers intently. I don't think he knew what the creds were exactly, but he kept staring at them. Right then, I felt eyeballs drilling holes in the back of my head. I looked behind me and just knew that I was about to be surrounded by a whole tribe of bona fide Taliban fighters.

I began to twitch all over as I looked around at all the foreigners, which made me feel like I had a squirrel in my knickers. But I guess it was really me who was the foreigner.

When we finally got through the lines, we walked toward the front of the concourse and were suddenly engulfed in a crowd of hundreds of Pakistanis there to meet their families or drop off passengers. It was total chaos. I dug around in my pockets to try and feel my passport and creds, discovering that they were gone. Just at that moment, I felt a tap on my shoulder and turned around to see that toothy guy smiling at me. I looked up at his hand, which he waved in the air, and low and behold, I saw my creds and passport. I watched as he and his friends had a good laugh about this dumb infidel and boy did I deserve it. I had visions of teletypes dancing in the air trying to explain why Osama carried my passport and creds as he tried to get through Customs in Miami. What a relief. That was one of every agent's worst nightmares.

We pushed through the crowd. I was a little uncomfortable as we were Westerners, unarmed, and in a tightly packed crowd of people, not like anything I had been around in Texas. But they were nice enough, especially that toothy guy. We climbed aboard Rick's SUV and headed off to the Serena Hotel. We only had five hours to rest and then had to return to the airport to board a flight to Kabul, Afghanistan. I showered, shaved, and had my clothes cleaned, but was not able to sleep before we left again.

We traveled to the airport once again and awaited our flight in a lounge, which served hot tea and cookies. It was pretty plain and Spartan, but the folks who worked there were polite. It was an oversized room, filled with a few old tables and old 1960s era kitchenette chairs. We chose to sit on one of the two dated sofas that surrounded a beaten coffee table. A very nervous Pakistani girl walked over to us and offered us tea and cookies. I don't think she dealt with many bruiser-looking dudes like us. She probably encountered a lot of wealthy Pakistani businessman, civilian do-gooders, the UN, or people from our own Department of State. We were a frightful sight. The tea was slightly warm, but was greatly appreciated.

Our plane arrived, so we said our goodbyes to Rick before we left the concourse. This flight was going to be an adventure in itself. The plane was a 1960 vintage Russian prop plane with metal seats and an interesting crew. The United Nations had chartered it for flights between Islamabad and Kabul. Rough ride, no frills—Air Russia.

We flew over the vast desolate mountains of the Hindu Kush that stretch across the border between Pakistan and Afghanistan. I could not help but think of Osama bin Laden, secreted somewhere in these same mountains, as we were buffeted by the wind currents that whipped through the highest peaks.

The plane was filled with foreigners, mostly UN employees, foreign soldiers, contractors, and US State Department employees. Frankly, I would have felt safer on a tightrope over a boiling cauldron of oil than on this old rickety plane. We passed over the edge of a long string of high peaks, and suddenly before us lay Kabul lying in an extensive, flat, barren valley surrounded by towering snow-capped mountains.

The city initially appeared as it probably did thousands of years ago, a vast maze of interconnected adobe compounds, woven together with a thread of dirt roads that led to the more congested city. There were pockets of compounds, ramshackle wooden huts, and old bombed-out buildings. We gazed over the city as we circled above the airport and saw a mass of cars crammed into the streets, fighting for every inch of broken pavement or dirt.

BUCKETS OF WATER

The antiquated plane circled the Kabul International Airport—boy, is that an overstatement—which gave us a clear view of the runway. The runway was encrusted with old, rusted Russian tanks, personnel carriers, and an interesting collection of trucks and armored vehicles. All had been left behind and pushed aside by a great war between nations, warlords, and religious zealots. These implements of war were strewn all about the cities, mountains, valleys, and deserts of Afghanistan and were a constant reminder of the devastation the Afghan people had experienced.

We landed and taxied up to the airport, parking shy of the entrance. Abboud Asad, an Afghan investigator and in-country facilitator employed by DEA, greeted us. He took our passports and walked us into the airport from the tarmac. Passengers lined up inside the empty terminal at the customs window. Asad walked to the door of the customs booth, bypassing all of the people standing in line, and handed our passports to the agent. Asad was one heck of a facilitator. I learned later that Asad had eight kids who lived away from him due to the threat of retaliation against him because of his work with the Americans. I loved this guy. We were of the same mind and heart. Asad loved his family and would sacrifice anything for their wellbeing. Surely his living and working in a war zone to provide for his family was a testament to that. Additionally, he was a good-natured soul, but careful in his approach to some who would take advantage. He was street smart and a good businessman, turning many a lemon into lemonade.

The customs agent thumbed through the pages and quickly stamped our passports, moving on to the next passenger waiting in line. I could smell the strong odor of urine throughout the terminal and soon discovered the plumbing in the restroom was not working. This became a pattern in all of the buildings in Afghanistan, those fortunate enough even to have an interior restroom. Open sewage systems were the prevalent means for waste disposal. Working water systems were a luxury. Most restaurants used buckets of water to rinse one's hands before and after meals.

We walked past a few Afghan Interior Ministry guards in their olive green uniforms, and they were armed with AK-47s—Russian Kalashnikovs. Outside the airport, families were waiting for their relatives. As we exited the airport, the DEA Country Attaché, John O' Rourke, met us. DEA has offices around the world, and in each country, an Attaché is assigned to direct their operations in their respective countries. His most difficult assignment is keeping the suits (management) off our backs.

John walked up to us and introduced himself. He had known Frank a long time. Frank used to work for John in Orlando, Florida before John accepted the assignment in Afghanistan. John carried himself in a deliberate manner, not stopping for pleasantries. He opened the back of a black, armored Chevrolet Suburban, reached inside, and handed Frank and me two sub-machineguns and two semi-automatic pistols.

I turned my head and watched the airport as we pulled away in the vehicle. Painted on the front wall of the terminal was the portrait of Ahmed Massoud, a national hero of Afghanistan and the legendary leader of the Northern Alliance who led the fight against the Taliban. Two Al Qaeda suicide bombers posing as a news crew killed Massoud. This happened a few months before the US started whacking Taliban.

RUBBER GUN SQUAD

We left the parking area of the airport and were suddenly engulfed in a crushing mass of vehicles. Asad maneuvered the armored truck through the traffic like his hair was on fire as he made his way to the US embassy.

As we drove towards the embassy, it became apparent that we

were indeed in one of the poorest nations on this earth. Devastatingly poor. Small children ran freely in the streets, along with yaks, cows, cars, buses, horses, and bicycles. Maimed or burned children stood at the curbside selling useless things. There were few police to watch the intersections and guide the traffic, which created mass confusion everywhere. Beggars peppered the street corners to reach out to the passing cars, which drove recklessly in total disregard of the beggars' safety. We passed by makeshift shops with fly-coated sections of goats and cows hanging from the rafters in the warm weather. The streets leading to the embassy were lined with dilapidated, pockmarked, and bombed out buildings—a parting gift from the Russian invasion and occupation.

The embassy compound seemed to be hastily constructed of makeshift concrete exterior walls, which surrounded the main building built in the 1970s and sixty or so trailers for living and offices. It was topped with concertina wire and guarded by battle-hardened Marines who just came over from Iraq. These Marines replaced the Marine Security Detachment, normally used to protect American embassies around the world. The Marines were thorough in their effort to provide all of us a secure place to sleep and work on our mission.

At first, it appeared that the Marines were a standoffish bunch. I later learned why. Members of the US State Department, US AID (Agency for International Development), and other members of our government elite were not very warm and fuzzy towards the Marines or members of law enforcement. The Marines were mostly young men and did not seem to garner much respect from the State Department. I don't understand why. My son fought in three tours in Iraq, and I know what he went through. He may have had the appearance of a boy on the outside, but I knew what lay beneath. A man hardened by war. I looked at these young Marines with a soft heart, like they were each my own son. Without these men protecting us, we were more than likely going to get whacked by some drive-by jihadist. And then there was DEA. We carried pistols in our leg holsters and machine guns draped off our necks as we walked around the compound, so I guess we were a little intimidating

After a few days, the Marines figured out who we were. I guess all the DEA ball caps, pens, and booty I passed out to them gave them a clue that we were not your normal bureaucrats. But what they enjoyed the most was a snappy insult directed toward a snooty bureaucrat, just out of the exalted one's earshot. This always got a chuckle and a warm smile from any Marine who overheard.

The State Department restricted anyone from walking around the embassy compound with loaded weapons. Imagine that, restricting weapons in the middle of a war zone. The constant loading and unloading of weapons as we left and returned to the embassy was burdensome and increased the likelihood of an accidental discharge. We were accustomed to carrying armed weapons, and this put our lives in jeopardy. The reaction time under fire is increased by valuable moments when an agent has to consider if his weapon is loaded or unloaded when fired upon. Later attacks on the embassy by terror groups validated this concern.

It made us all feel like the Keystone Kops, armed with an empty revolver or a rubber gun. The friction between the US State Department and DEA was so thick you could cut it with a knife. They demanded operational authority over us, and we, of course, ignored them. This became more pronounced as we became more successful. We moved in stealth under the ever-watchful eye of the State Department.

Another restriction imposed by the State Department was the requirement that we travel in numbers (at least four armed agents) due to the high incidence of attacks. We only had three agents, and then two when Frank was sent to northern Afghanistan to Bagram, an American air base. We did not allow this to restrict our movement. Several of the task forces came out of Bagram, including air operations, in support of Operation Enduring Freedom throughout Afghanistan.

We both missed Frank when he left. Frank was disappointed as he came to Afghanistan to hang out with his bud John. But the mission required one of us to go north. He adapted and really got along with the US Army Criminal Investigation Task Force he hung out with and cut a wide swath while he was there. John had to settle for an old fart like me. Oh well, the rigors of war. I felt as if John carried the weight of the world on his shoulders. He had to deal constantly with the State Department and DEA Headquarters as he tried to get us support.

We lacked adequate weapons, protective gear, and communication. You know, all that "stuff" we were promised. It was like they dropped us off in the war and forgot about us. John, a great communicator, though quiet when left to his own, managed to grease the skids of bureaucracy with the ease of an Irishman caught with his hands in the cookie jar. John used these skills to aid me in my assignments as well. One of my duties was to establish an elite Afghan Counter-Narcotics group to work throughout the country. I guess "elite" was more wishful thinking, but it looked good on the teletypes we sent to HQ. John fought hard to cut through the bureaucratic red tape and obtain funding for them. The members of this group, the previously unemployed bicycle shop owners and sheepherders, were untrained and inexperienced, but emboldened and eager to learn. They began with five borrowed pistols. Their hearts were right, but we had to start from scratch. Bless their hearts. John never stopped trying to make all of our lives easier and safer, against the greatest of odds.

During the course of our day-to-day activities, we traveled about in armored vehicles, meeting informants, and locating remote mountain heroin labs and fortresses protected by Afghan warlords. Wherever we went, we felt eyes studying our every move. DEA was in town, and everyone knew it.

Sometimes we traveled alone, because there was no one else to ride shotgun. I would leave John at the office and hit the road with Asad or just by myself when Asad was tied up. When out and about with Asad, or alone, I ran a risk. Ever the risk taker, like all DEA boys, I thrived on the adrenaline. (What the State Department did not know, we of course did not tell them.) I really liked hanging out with Asad. He was the fixer. He could make anything happen—and did. In our free time, which was rare, he would take me out and show me the town. Asad said that the once-green valleys of years past are now dust bowls because the Russians destroyed their irrigation systems and cut down all the trees in retaliation for insurgent attacks during their occupation. When we drove through those desolate lands, I could only imagine what beauty must have once thrived there. What remained was mile after mile of dry, harsh deserts, bald mountains, and rock.

The rural areas are as they were three thousand years ago with nomads living in tents and shepherds watching their sheep. How these people live and survive with so few means is beyond me. People sat around in the middle of the plains, or walked with nothing in sight. No water anywhere. I could see that they were a tough people.

The Afghans were now free from the oppression of the Taliban that replaced the occupation of the Russians. But it will not last, despite their best efforts. Time and war will cause them to forget the frying pan they jumped out of with our help. One day they will invite back the Taliban, believing it to be safer than the fire that consumes them today. A dog returns to his vomit.

CHAPTER SEVEN

CIRCLE THE WAGONS

DANGER IN PARADISE

On December 28, 2003, a homicide bomber was apprehended by members of the Afghan National Directorate of Security (NDS) near the Kabul International Airport in Kabul Afghanistan and detonated a bomb (improvised explosive device), killing five of their agents. These Afghan security agents were the Afghan counterparts of our own American CIA agents. The Russian KGB had trained the agents of the NDS during their occupation, and we supplemented it when we moved in.

The bomb scene was investigated, and it was determined that the bomb was made from an Iranian pressure cooker stuffed to the gills with high explosives. Little did we know that we would later have a close encounter with this same kind of device and the same bomb maker. Investigation by the Afghan NDS agents, the American CIA, and the FBI failed to determine the group responsible for this heinous act.

In the spring of 2004, rumors began to circulate among coalition intelligence agencies in Kabul about a ten member Chechen terrorist cell that operated somewhere within the city. It was reported that this cell was responsible for killing these Afghan agents. No one was able to confirm this, and FBI and other intelligence agencies doubted its existence. It turned out to be a rabbit trail, leading the investigators to nowhere. The investigation of the murder of the Afghan agents eventually was shelved. The intelligence agencies were already overburdened with stopping more imminent threats, so they put it on the back burner.

WHISTLING IN THE DARK

On April 5, I got a call from the Marines at the front gate. One of our sources had arrived and wanted to meet with us. I walked to the gated embassy entrance to meet the source, a former Taliban commander and suspected member of Al Qaeda.

We had been working with this guy for a few months. His job was to locate heroin labs scattered throughout the canyons of the Hindu Kush Mountains. Let's just call him Mustafa. Mustafa looked like a killer and was indeed a killer. Scarred from head to toe, he was reputed to have whacked a lot of Russians in days gone by. After attending Al Qaeda training camps, he looked around and figured the retirement package for terrorists wasn't all that great. He studied his options and decided we would pay more. Mustafa had a winning smile, and we understood each other. He liked the money, and we liked the heroin we were able to seize because of his help. We walked Mustafa to the secure trailer to debrief him. He looked serious. Normally, we would engage Mustafa with a little small talk first, but he got right to his purpose for being there. He said that he had a friend who had recently traveled to Kabul from eastern Afghanistan. This guy was also a former Taliban commander, and Mustafa had known him for many years. To protect his identity, we will call him Ahmed. He said that his friend, Ahmed, currently lived with friends in a compound in the Chilestoon neighborhood located in southeast Kabul.

Chilestoon was a rough neighborhood. Just a few days before our meeting with Mustafa, four Westerners had backpacked through Afghanistan on vacation and happened upon this wonderful, quaint neighborhood. These wonderful, warm-hearted Chilestoonians, ever so welcoming to strangers (especially infidels), ran out to greet them. They surrounded these Europeans, hog tied the two men, and stoned them to death. The females who accompanied them on this romp in a war zone were never seen again. I couldn't wait to go to this neighborhood; in fact, I was giddy with excitement! Soon I hoped I would come with many more friends carrying guns that go bang. Shame on these rats that devour our innocent.

Ahmed told Mustafa that the "friends" in the compound were an active terror cell that manufactured bombs and sold them to Hesb Islami Gulbidden (HIG) and the Taliban. HIG is another radical jihadist group of terrorists who have sided with Osama bin Laden and are fighting our troops in Afghanistan. Mustafa said that his friend, Ahmed, wanted to make some dough, and I'm not talking about flat bread here. He heard from Mustafa that we paid big bucks for this kind of intelligence, and he wanted a piece of the action. We told Mustafa that we wanted to meet with him and soon.

We gave Mustafa a GPS (Global Positioning System), which was the size of a small cell phone, and told Mustafa to give it to his friend Ahmed. We intended to download the coordinates from Mustafa's GPS, locate the terror cell compound, and have our friends with guns hit it before any more attacks by these rats could be mounted. We instructed him to have Ahmed take it with him, trigger it (register the coordinates) when he was at the compound, and then bring it to us when we next met him. We also told Mustafa to let us know if these terrorists were going to attack. Mustafa left.

A few days later, we got a call from Mustafa. Mustafa told us that Ahmed had the coordinates of the compound and would meet us by the King's Tomb, which was on a hillside overlooking Kabul. Now the King's Tomb is a scene right out of a classic horror film of the 1940s. To drive to the King's Tomb, you must drive along a steep, hillside gravel road with a sheer drop off that leads up to the tomb, the burial place of the last King of Afghanistan, Nadir Shah, who was assassinated in 1933. It is desolate and secluded, but surrounded by the city of Kabul. On top of the hill are hundreds, if not thousands of graves, stacked stones, sticks with flags, black and green, marking the graves of both heroes and villains who fell in these wars.

The night's city lights gently illuminate the neighborhoods of Kabul and can be seen from the King's Tomb. The King's Tomb is a large domed mosaic encrusted building, pock-marked from all of the cursed wars that followed the King's death and plagued his people. The King's wife and members of his immediate family are also buried beneath the tomb in a damp, cavernous, concrete-walled room.

We drove to the hilltop with Mustafa in our armored Chevy Suburban. As we waited for Ahmed to arrive, we could hear the flags flapping in the wind, hidden from our sight by the darkness. All I could think about was the boogeyman. I mean, for all we knew, Mustafa had set us up and maybe some Taliban SWAT team was going to come kill us all. Yeah, or even just hit us with an RPG or something worse. Maybe the walking dead or some axe murderer was going to jump in the SUV with us and hack us all to pieces. Okay, Sellers. Get a grip. It was just spooky—real spooky.

Suddenly, we saw a dark figure emerge from the shadows of the graveyard. We studied the dark figure as it slowly walked towards us. Mustafa quietly, reverently whispered to me that it was Ahmed. Man, what a creepy entrance, but I have to admit, Ahmed had the style and the gonads to walk from that graveyard cloaked in darkness. His entrance was foreboding and theatrical. What a stud.

As he came closer to the SUV, he became more visible. He was tall, handsome with a long black beard, and well heeled. He got in the SUV, and after a brief introduction, we began to question him about his friends. Ahmed was a very stern and deliberate man. I recognized immediately that he was accustomed to being treated with respect. He truly had a commanding presence. He did not mince words. Frankly, I think he would have killed any one of us, if the price was right. We knew that he was there for the money. I don't think we could have bought Ahmed ourselves, but I sensed that we could rent him for a while.

Ahmed confirmed that his friends in the compound had bragged to him about killing the Afghan NDS security agents and had prepared more suicide bombs for use by the Taliban and HIG against the Americans. I believed him. I knew he would deliver. Ahmed did not like the infidel, but had a taste for fine clothes and no telling what else.

He handed the GPS over to us. Ahmed said that there were several members of the terror cell living in the compound, along with women and children. He explained that the terror cell made bombs from old Russian artillery rounds and armed them for detonation. Ahmed confirmed that the bombs were sold to the Taliban and HIG who gave them to suicide bombers for use throughout Kabul and the surrounding area.

Ahmed said the leader of this group, Ashraf, claimed to have been responsible for killing five Afghan security agents in December and was involved in ongoing suicide bomber attacks against American and coalition forces. Ashraf sent out zealot suicide bombers to attack our forces under the direction of both Taliban and HIG forces. Ashraf's base of operations was his compound in the Chilestoon neighborhood.

We told Ahmed to return to the compound and keep a watchful eye. If they gave any indication of moving on a target, he was to let us know. He left the vehicle and walked, no, I dare say *disappeared* into the darkness, just as he arrived. It gave me the willies.

We returned to the office and downloaded the GPS for what we hoped were the stored coordinates of the terrorist compound. Alas, there were none. For some reason unbeknownst to us, either the GPS or Ahmed had failed. We talked to Mustafa, and he insisted that Ahmed knew how to use the GPS and that there had to be a reason for it to not have registered the coordinates. The answer was simple, but unknown to us at that time. We learned later that Ahmed triggered the GPS while he stood under an extended roof outside the front door of the compound, which blocked the GPS from reaching the satellites.

WAKE ME UP WHEN THE WAR IS OVER

On April 17, 2004, a new agent was assigned to the Kabul country office. Jeffery Higgins was an experienced, aggressive agent from Boston, but worked out of the New York City Office. He never ceased to let me know he was not a New Yorker, but a Bostonian. Something about those darn Yankees.

Jeff was assigned to the DEA New York Field Division prior to the attack on the World Trade Center on September 11, 2001. He described it as a scene right out of a horror movie.

Thousands of people streamed out of the city on foot. The North Tower of the World Trade Center stood alone in the backdrop of the New York City skyline, smoking like a chimney. The North Tower collapsed into the rubble of the South Tower as Jeff made his way to the scene from the divisional field office.

Jeff was enveloped in the thick smoke that emitted from the carnage as he walked down the Westside Highway towards the fallen North Tower. Fireballs exploded through the newly formed caverns in the pavement as he continued on. Jeff and two others cops were the first to reach the fallen tower from the west side. They encountered and rendered aid to the many wounded victims, which were strewn about the wreckage. Nearby vehicles exploded and spewed flames as Jeff and the cops dug through the debris to search for more survivors. As Jeff stepped across the broken pieces of the remains of the tower, he peered into the holes beneath him and could see hundreds of feet below. It occurred to him that he could easily be killed if he wasn't careful in this field of crushed buildings. He focused as he pressed on and continued his search until ordered to pull back due to fears that more buildings were about to fall. Jeff refused to leave and forged through the many buildings that surrounded the crash site in his search for survivors.

His recollections of these events beckoned him to put in for Afghanistan when DEA asked for volunteers. Hidden in Jeff's heart were the memories of that day, and little did he know that within days of his arrival in Afghanistan, he would have his chance to bring a little American justice to these jihadists. Neither, of course, did I.

Jeff never seemed to be downbeat and was always positive about life. If he had a middle name, it would be "I'm bored...Let's go kill some Taliban." When Asad and I met him, we looked at each other and just sighed. Jeff was definitely high speed and really was cut out for this war stuff. Jeff and I became quick friends.

Around him, I was truly amazed. He always wanted to run off to Jalalabad, sixty miles north of Kabul, through the Taliban-infested foothills in the Hindu Kush. I dissuaded him with concerns that there were no five star hotels there and I would have to bathe in buckets of dirty water, not to mention the fact that we might wake up with a butter knife necktie. Undaunted, he never ceased to seek out more adventures. He was one real gunfighter. Mr. Joe Tactical.

Shortly after Jeff's arrival in Afghanistan, we were all invited to the home of the Afghan Drug Czar for dinner. Some big shots from DEA headquarters and the American Drug Czar were in town on April 20, 2004 to assess the situation in Afghanistan.

Jeff did not want to go, but I called dibs on staying behind to man the fort. As I said, this ain't my first rodeo, and if you snooze, you lose. I had no interest in hob-knobbing and welcomed the opportunity to kick back. Who wants to dress up and go spend their evening nervously navigating through conversations with a bunch of big Kahunas? I wore a suit once for my wife a few years ago on our anniversary, and I didn't plan on repeating the experience any time soon. I was anxious for them to leave before they got wise to my wiggling, and much to my relief, they left early to get across town. I snickered at Jeff as he left with the big shots, thankful that I dodged that bullet.

I looked around our empty office and realized that there were no watchful eyes for the first time in several days. I told myself, "Self, wake me up when the war is over." I kicked back, put my feet up on the desk, sighed contentedly, and nodded off. The phone rang loudly, almost knocking me out of my chair. It was the Marines at the front gate. Apparently, they didn't care about my plans.

Mustafa had arrived and wanted to meet with us. Stirred from my slumber, I looked around and remembered that all my friends had left me. I called downstairs to the Marine Anti-Terrorist Intelligence Cell (ATIC) who were based at the embassy and hooked up with a few of the Marines. ATIC is a proactive unit of Marine intelligence agents responsible for protecting the embassy from threats. Their job was to scour the city outside of the embassy and gather any intelligence on threats to the embassy itself.

We walked to the gated embassy entry to meet Mustafa and escort him through security. We brought Mustafa to the secure trailer to debrief him. I introduced the Marine intel boys to Mustafa and asked him to begin. He was contacted by Ahmed and said that the group of terrorists were going to deliver a bomb to a suicide bomber at the downtown Blue Mosque. This delivery was to take place at 5:30 pm.

I looked at my watch. It was 5:00 pm.

The bomb maker, Abdul Shaheed, and Ahmed were to deliver the IED, armed with a detonation device that would be in the pocket of his vest. Ahmed said that he was to be the handler for the suicide bomber and guide him to the target. He believed Americans to be the target, but Shaheed would have the details. He described the bomb as an Iranian pressure cooker, stuffed with high explosives and metal objects for shrapnel. The Marines and I exchanged glances—Ahmed could not have known that this was the exact type of device used against the five security agents who were killed, as this information was not released to the public. It suddenly dawned on me that Abdul Shaheed probably constructed the first bomb used to kill the five Afghan agents as well. It was at that moment that I realized my night just got a whole lot more interesting.

There was no time for protocol. We had to move fast. I quickly considered the possibilities for help in the operation, but my options were limited. I notified the FBI and other intelligence agencies of the possibility of this terrorist cell operating in Kabul, but they felt it was not credible. They had given me their blessing to work the case as they were already buried in operations. The Marine intelligence officer called the US military for assistance. The US military deferred to coalition forces charged with the security of Kabul. Political ramifications had to be considered. All matters of security within the boundaries of the city of Kabul had to be turned over to the coalition.

Coalition forces, with members from approximately thirty-one countries, were organized as the International Security Assistance

Force (ISAF). Kabul was divided into sections, with different coalition countries assigned to secure each section. US military passed this pending attack intelligence to ISAF for their action.

There was little time to stand up an immediate response by ISAF, but efforts were made, with the US military acting in a support role. ISAF promised to send out a Quick Reaction Force (the Canadian Special Forces) to secure the bomb maker and bomber when I located them. This meant going outside of the wire (leaving the safety of the embassy compound) with Mustafa and a small contingent of Marines. All of the DEA boys were at the shindig, hob-knobbing, so I had to go it alone without them.

At first, I assumed the Marines would go with me to cover the meet, but was told by the chief that they were on "restriction." The bureaucrat in charge of the embassy refused to let them leave the compound. The Marines had upset members of the US State Department with their aggressive tactics while they gathered intelligence in the community. So the Marines were out, and I had to go solo with the snitch. We were burning daylight, and I was anxious to get going before we lost our chance to catch the bomber.

ISAF called and said that the Canadians were being mobilized. I knew that we didn't have the luxury of waiting for them, as I feared that the IED would be delivered to another terrorist. I left with Mustafa and drove to the Blue Mosque. I told the Marines that I would radio in the location of the meet and drop him in the laps of the Canadian Quick Reaction Force.

THE BLUE MOSQUE

Mustafa and I drove at breakneck speeds to the intersection near the Pul Kishty mosque in the Sar-E-Drove neighborhood. The Pul

Kishty mosque dome was painted bright blue and stood out amongst the drab surroundings, thus the handle "Blue Mosque." Our time was running out. We had to find Shaheed before the delivery was made.

The streets were crowded with people, as the Blue Mosque had just let out from their afternoon prayer. There were hundreds of vehicles and thousands of people who jammed the traffic circle and streets leading into the mosque. I dropped off Mustafa and drove around the traffic circle. We spotted Ahmed, who waited near the Blue Mosque for the arrival of Shaheed, the bomb maker. Mustafa spotted Shaheed in the crowd and signaled to me.

Ahmed stood outside a bombed-out building as crowds of people scurried about him unaware of the meeting that was about to take place. Suddenly, a shorter male walked up to Ahmed carrying a plastic grocery sack with a large object in it. They exchanged greetings and began to pace back and forth as they talked. Shaheed would stop from time to time to look about as if he expected someone to arrive. He was indeed.

Shaheed awaited the arrival of the suicide bomber. The bomber would take possession of the bomb, receive his instructions from Shaheed, and leave with Ahmed (as his guide) to commit the ultimate act of jihad against some unsuspecting American soldiers at the nearby post.

I called in to the Marines and reported the arrival of the bomb maker. Protocol required that the Canadians apprehend the bomb maker and suicide bomber because the area around the Blue Mosque was in their jurisdiction. As I waited for their arrival, I photographed the meeting and tried to avoid detection. I hoped that the Canadians would come quickly and figured it would take them thirty minutes, max, to mount up and ride like the wind to the Blue Mosque.

It was 6:15 pm, forty-five minutes after I had notified ISAF, and still no Quick Reaction Force. I started to think that maybe it was a

SRF—you know, a "Slow Reaction Force." Hoping it was at least that, I had to wait. It would be suicide to attempt an arrest at this time. I was armed with a machine gun and a pistol, but was surrounded by thousands of Afghans who may not take too kindly to an old honky slamming an Afghan to the pavement. So I figured it was the better part of valor to wait for the Canadians.

I continued to drive around the traffic circle, which was jammed with people and cars, as I kept a watchful eye on the meeting. It began to get a little obvious to a traffic cop as I continued round and round the circle. I figured I had better change it up a bit and tried to conceal my vehicle in a mess of vehicles parked haphazardly along the street. It did not take long for the crowds and the police to spot me, a Westerner in a Toyota SUV with US embassy plates. I kind of stuck out like a cracker in a bowl of soup. The surrounding Afghans gathered up with the policeman leading the pack and began to walk towards my SUV. Not wanting a confrontation with the meet going down just yards away, I skedaddled.

I resumed going around the traffic circle and up and down the street, watching and waiting for the second terrorist to show up. Shaheed had a firm grasp on the grocery sack with the IED inside as he waited with my source. Time was passing.

It was 7:15 pm, and I began to realize that it was an NRF—"No Reaction Force." I looked up and down the street to no avail. I called the Marines and found out that the Canadians weren't coming. I weighed in my mind whether I should commit suicide as well and make a run on Shaheed. I could round up Mustafa and together with Ahmed throw Shaheed in the back of my G-ride, but I came to my senses. What idiot would manhandle a suicide bomber? Better, I sought out another vantage point to squeeze off a round into his head. I drove past them and parked behind a double-parked taxi with no driver. Sliding across to the passenger seat, I pulled my machine gun from the floorboard and readied it to crank a double tap in Shaheed's think box before getting out of Dodge.

Suddenly Shaheed and Ahmed began to walk away from the intersection. They moved at a fast gait and disappeared into the crowds. I learned later that Shaheed had tired of waiting for the suicide bomber to show and left. I guess it was Shaheed's lucky day. Probably a good thing for me as well. My intel was strong that Shaheed carried a bomb and detonator, but anytime you get tactical, you got a lot of "'splaining to do, Lucy." I drove to ISAF headquarters without the bomber.

NORWEGIANS ARE COOL

At ISAF headquarters, I met with Canadian Major McLean, who headed the Intelligence Section. I updated him on the operation. He told me that they had attempted to act but failed due to time constraints and other problems that surfaced. ISAF command had called a meeting with all of the nations represented by their military commanders. Each nation of the coalition had their own contingent of soldiers, and though they had autonomy, they reported to a single coalition leader, who was routinely rotated between the nations. All security issues regarding the city of Kabul had to be dealt with by this council.

Major McLean and I walked over to the doublewide air-conditioned trailer that served as the conference room. I looked around and saw military uniforms from a few dozen countries mill around the room as Major McLean offered me a chair. American Brigadier General Les Fuller, a career Special Forces officer, walked quietly and with authority into the conference room. He sucked out all the oxygen of the room, and the conversations cut off mid-sentence. Everyone snapped to attention and saluted him as he cut a wide swath to the head of the conference table. He sat down at the head of the very large oblong wooden table, looked into the now-seated array of uniforms, and succinctly asked what had happened.

It was his time in the bubble (leadership rotation) as the commander of ISAF forces. General Fuller listened patiently as he was briefed by Major McLean and two or three other foreign military representatives. The major explained that upon notification and the request for assistance by the US military, they contacted Ottawa and requested permission to stand up the reaction force. Ottawa took its sweet time considering it; about an hour had passed before they finally decided to throw its full support behind a declination to assist.

I guess things move a little slower up there due to the cold weather, or maybe they just didn't want to play. Either way, it was too late for another country to commit and stand up another reaction force. Time had run out. Major McLean was a good guy and more than a little embarrassed. I felt for him, knowing we all are subject to the direction of bureaucratic stupidvisors and are helpless to counterman their self-serving mandates.

General Fuller was disappointed in the ISAF failure to respond and spoke in no uncertain terms that I risked my life on this operation and was left alone because of their inability to raise a reaction force. In 2004, ISAF was still working out the kinks and relied heavily on the US military for guidance. He looked over to me and asked what the next move was going to be.

I had debriefed Mustafa prior to the meet with ISAF and learned that all was not lost. Apparently, Shaheed was angered by the failure of the bomber to show up and said that he would himself commit jihad against the Americans by detonating the bomb. Shaheed told Ahmed to meet him near the stadium in Kabul the following morning at 8:00 am. Shaheed would either deliver the bomb to the bomber or do the bombing himself. Ahmed would once again serve as a handler and ensure that the mission was completed. It was apparent that Shaheed wanted to see this thing through. Ahmed would facilitate it, guiding Shaheed or the bomber to the target, the American military base. The delivery of the IED was to take place at a small teahouse near the stadium (infamous for executions by the Taliban).

General Fuller was visibly pleased that we still had a dog in this fight and ordered his staff to provide whatever support was necessary to get the job done. He studied the country representatives for a few moments before he asked for a volunteer to set up a reaction force for the morning operation. It was apparent that the next reaction force had better react or someone was going to be peeling potatoes in the mess hall. The Norwegian Special Forces commander stood up and volunteered to be the lead action element for the operation on the ground, and the Dutch Special Forces said they would cover the operation with air support. The general promised me support for the operation the following day and commanded ISAF to begin preparations.

Lt. Col. Chris Costa, the Chief of the Human Intelligence Branch at Central Command, represented the US military and provided us the top cover we needed to keep the Supremes off our backs while we were running and gunning in the streets of Kabul. Chris worked for Central Command and only served as an advisor to ISAF on occasion. Chris and General Fuller went way back, and he had a lot of confidence in Chris. Because of this, Chris was given a lot of latitude in working with ISAF in this operation.

Chris stayed behind with me at ISAF and helped formulate the tactical operation with his counterparts in the coalition. Chris and his chief intelligence agent, Stan Maleski, would be with the ISAF command at the Kabul Multi-National Brigade headquarters across town in west Kabul during the operation in order to keep the operation on track and monitor our safety. Stan was a good man and very knowledgeable of the ongoing insurgent activities in Kabul. Though ISAF commanded the operation, Chris was the conduit to communicate with our operational unit and Dutch air support. Chris and I both heard murmurs of skepticism from some of the other agencies (not in attendance) that doubted the veracity of our sources, which we saw as an opportunity to proceed without concern of outside interference.

The best way to describe Chris is to say that he is the kind of guy you want giving orders when things get rough. He had to weigh the political pitfalls of keeping various countries from fighting with each other while at the same time work to ensure a successful operation. He had the job nobody wanted, but we were all glad he stepped up to the plate. We knew he could handle any pitch thrown at him.

Following the conclusion of the meeting, I walked over and introduced myself to this pale, Nordic-looking dude from Norway. (I am one to talk; I am so white that when I take off my shirt you can see my liver.) I felt confident that these Norwegian guys were on top of their game. I mean, isn't Norway where the Vikings came from?

"Thanks for volunteering. I'm Tim. Are you guys pumped to get this guy?"

"Ja, ja! This is our first mission."

I was a little surprised and asked, "Your first mission in Afghanistan?"

He clarified with a little smile: "Oh no, no. It's our first mission in over two hundred years—outside of Norway."

I fell silent for a moment as I mulled over the ramifications of what he just said. I didn't want to be responsible for them returning to Norway with the first failed operation in a couple of centuries under their belts. Oh boy.

CHAPTER EIGHT

THE LAST STAND

THE TEAHOUSE

On April 21 at 7:00 am, we met at the ISAF HQ and formulated the operations plan. The Norwegians left and set up a strike platform near the teahouse. I left with an interpreter, SA Jeff Higgins, the Marine ATIC intel chief, the source, and a Norwegian communications soldier.

We rode in a Ford Explorer. I was in the front seat, the Marine in the driver's seat, the source Ahmed and the interpreter (an American of Afghan descent) in the middle, with Jeff and the Norwegian in the rear compartment. We drove to set up near the teahouse.

The teahouse was as small as a shed, wooden, nasty, and with a mound of dirt in the center of the small room embedded with an open fire. Afghans would sit and drink tea, warming themselves by the fire while talking about the latest trends in burkas. You know—light blue, lighter blue, or the latest craze—a blue burka with a hint of grey blue. There was only enough room for three to four people inside. The teahouse was crammed in a long corridor of ramshackle shops. It was situated along the Kabul River, which flowed kind of like peanut butter and was filled with a lot of trash and small goats.

The day was dark with thunderclouds that burst erratically

throughout the morning. The rain pushed the floating dust in the air to the ground and created puddles of brown water in the lowest points of the roads. Open ditches that lined the side of the roads served as open sewers for the neighborhoods. The open sewers filled with rainwater and overflowed into the streets. Crowds of people scurried about seemingly with some direction in mind.

We parked our vehicle and waited along the street near an entry leading to the dirt road that coursed alongside the river. This road was encrusted with debris along one side of the river and had several dozen shops of similar construction as the teahouse. I guess you could call it a strip mall. Sort of.

I don't know how the wind did it, but between showers from the thunderstorms, the dust kicked back up and floated around like a heavy veil, obscuring the shops and people lollygagging around. What a nasty place for a meet. It was very difficult to get to the teahouse with the armored vehicles without screaming that we were coming.

We were only blocks from Afghanistan's Presidential Palace, the US embassy, US military, ISAF headquarters, and other more sensitive areas. We were greatly concerned that one of these locations might also be Shaheed's target. There were a lot of Americans who stood between him and his seventy-two virgins (or is it one, seventy-two-year-old cranky virgin? I'm not sure). Near the entrances of many of these facilities were dozens of soldiers of all nationalities, US Army military police, and Marines guarding the post and the US embassy. There were also civilian contractors and government employees traversing in and out of the secured facilities. Target rich.

We waited. Minutes later, Ahmed's phone rang. It was Shaheed. He had arrived in the area and was en route to the teahouse. We dropped off Ahmed, who walked to the teahouse to wait for Shaheed and instructed him to call us when Shaheed showed up. We waited for well over an hour when we got the call from Ahmed. Shaheed had arrived, and he had the bomb in his possession. He carried the IED, an explosive-laden pressure cooker in a plastic grocery sack. Shaheed had the remote-controlled detonator in his vest. Ahmed told us that the IED was armed and ready to go. Giddy up! It was time to move on Shaheed before he had time to set his plan in motion.

We radioed the Norwegians who immediately set a perimeter around the shops and rushed to the teahouse in an armored personnel carrier. It was like an elephant walking through a thicket of bushes— loud, large, and slow going. We rushed in and got there just as the Norwegians pulled in. Heck, a blind man could have seen us coming. We scouted around, but the bomber was nowhere to be found. The bomber was gone. He was lost in the crowd. Nuts.

When all else fails, you kick the dog. We grabbed Ahmed, who was trying to blend in the crowd that had gathered around him, and threw him to the ground. We quickly arrested him and threw him in the back seat of the SUV. This was an age-old trick to conceal the fact that he worked for us. I asked him what happened. He cried out that Shaheed was there, but saw the Norwegians coming and fled.

We told him to call Shaheed on his mobile phone and ask him where he was. Shaheed answered the phone and said that he was across the river near the Blue Mosque. I told Ahmed to tell him to wait there and that he would come to him. Shaheed said that there were ISAF forces everywhere and he was going to get out of there. Shaheed said he would wait only five minutes before he would leave.

ACROSS THE KABUL RIVER

We immediately drove down the dirt road and headed to the only bridge within sight. Weaving in and out of the traffic, we darted over the bridge across the Kabul River. Our path was obstructed with cars, carts, and spectators watching the Norwegian operation, but we managed to break through. The nearby Eid Gha, the largest mosque in Afghanistan, had just let out and the devotees poured into the streets.

We pushed through the crowd to reach the Blue Mosque across the Kabul River from the Eid Gha mosque. When it became impossible to continue through the crowds, we told Ahmed to leave the car and run to the Blue Mosque to find Shaheed. He bolted from the car and ran in the direction of the mosque. I watched as he disappeared into the crowds and traffic. We were alone. The Norwegians were across the river quelling the crowd and still sought out Shaheed. I am sure they thought the operation was a bust and the bomber was in the wind, but continued their search in the shops and neighborhood that surrounded the teahouse. The crowds outside of the teahouse had gathered to rubberneck and had become unruly.

Our Norwegian communications dude who was jammed in the rear of the SUV chattered away, telling his command what we were up to. Jeff was with him, crammed into the tight cargo compartment.

Minutes later, our Ahmed reappeared in the crowd, and beside him was Shaheed. Shaheed carried a pinkish, plastic grocery sack that contained the pressure cooker. Ahmed had described it exactly. What a great snitch. We surely had found the perpetrators of that heinous murder of the five agents who started this hunt for the terror cell. We watched as they proceeded to walk towards us. There were so many people and vehicles in the streets along the river that we were able to blend in.

I asked the Marine to call command and request permission to bag the bomber. Heck, he was headed right towards us. The ISAF command center ordered us (through Chris) to stand down and wait for the Norwegians to arrive to make the arrest. I don't know who was more frustrated, Chris or us.

We did what command ordered and watched as Ahmed walked with Shaheed within yards of our vehicle. Jeff and I were pumped up. We chomped at the bit as we tried to hold back. We watched as Shaheed spun his head around to look hard for ISAF uniforms and vehicles. He never once noticed our G-ride with embassy plates filled to the brim with goons.

Poor Ahmed. He carefully guided Shaheed to within almost an arm's length of our truck. Ahmed expected us to leap from our vehicle and arrest Shaheed...we were cops and Marines, weren't we? But Ahmed did not know the political ramifications. ISAF forces had to make the arrest. No exceptions. They were responsible for security in Kabul and all of the individual commands watched this operation. This was their first real joint security operation of any significance, and all the individual commanders wanted to have a part in it if it was successful. If protocol were ignored, the foreign commands would have a hissy fit. Poor Chris was caught in the middle and tried to find an opening for us to act.

The Kabul River and thousands of Afghans separated us from the Norwegians and prevented them from responding. The bomber had to be stopped. We were all that stood between him and the American targets.

FLAPJACK

The bomber and Ahmed walked past a group of buses, which were dropping off people and picking them up. They turned around and began to head towards our vehicle again. It was apparent that Ahmed tried once again to steer him towards us. I asked the Marine for the phone and began giving Chris a play-by-play over the phone. Shaheed was within fifty yards...thirty yards...ten yards. I told him that we had to act. I knew Chris could not authorize it because he was bound by protocol. But I could sense his frustration as he relayed ISAF's order for us to stand down.

We wanted to arrest Shaheed before he got lost in the crowd. Five yards…Shaheed passed our vehicle. He was so close I could see the crusted breakfast in his beard.

The Norwegians across the river could not reach us. They were bottlenecked at the bridge, locked in traffic. Out of frustration, I handed the phone to the Marine. I wanted to free myself up to jet. Jeff was frustrated too. We wanted to bag this guy so bad and didn't care that we were violating protocol. We couldn't help it; we were old school agents with little regard for limitations.

Jeff squirmed in the back of the Explorer as he tried to position himself. I twisted around backwards in the front seat so I could follow Shaheed with my eyes as he walked past us. Ahmed gave up and walked directly into the surrounding crowd while Shaheed studied the area across the river trying to spot the Norwegians. Ahmed distanced himself from Shaheed and when Shaheed turned back around, Ahmed was gone.

Shaheed picked up his pace and darted into the crowd to look for Ahmed. Shaheed was gone as well, buried in a sea of Afghan pajamas. The Marine reported to command that we had lost Shaheed. We all yelled and moaned about losing him. We tried real hard to obey orders, but simultaneously cranked off about those same baloney orders to stand down. We had already lost him once, and we had him within our grips only to have to let him go. Where were those darn Norwegians?

Suddenly, while we were twisting and turning and spinning in our seats to try and spot Shaheed, he jettisoned from the crowd. He was alone. He had lost Ahmed and looked fearful, panicked. Shaheed still carried the IED in the opaque, pink plastic sack. When he bolted past our truck, we told Chris that he had found him. The Norwegians were still nowhere in sight, trapped across the river, tangled up in traffic as they tried to jam their way towards us.

Shaheed was a man on a mission. Ahead of him were a couple of buses loading up people. He was determined to get to those buses. His eyes were locked on the closest one's open door with a stack of people lined up to get on. He pressed towards the bus through the crowds and attached himself to the last guy in line waiting to board.

Jeff and I feared that Shaheed would commandeer the bus. Once on the bus, he could blow it up if we tried to stop it, or use the bus as a missile on nearby facilities. It was crunch time. I told the Marine to ask for orders to arrest Shaheed. I was finished with this deal. Everyone was yelling in the vehicle, and we were losing ground fast. I screamed back at Jeff, "Come on partner, let's go!" Before the Marine completed his request to command, I had bolted from the car. The Marine blurted out, "Sir, it's too late. DEA's out of the car."

Jeff was hung up in the cargo section, but broke free and bailed. We knew that if we did not stop him, Afghans would surely die, and if Shaheed reached his target, Americans or coalition forces were going to die as well.

Now this was not the brightest idea I ever had. Firstly, we had disobeyed a direct order from ISAF command to stand down. I hated to think of the consequences of that decision, so as usual I didn't think. Secondly, how in the heck do you stop a bomber? Shoot him? What if I missed and whacked an innocent Afghan? Shaheed had many innocents who surrounded him. I would have to claw my way through the crowds to get close enough to draw a bead on him. I had to do something and would figure it out on the way. I had at least two to three seconds before impact—and that was plenty of time.

I ran towards the bomber as I weaved in and out through the crowd at a fast clip. I didn't look behind me, but hoped Jeff had hooked up to my trailer hitch. When Jeff exited the truck, I was nowhere to be seen. He scanned the crowd that had swallowed up the bomber between the buses and us. He saw me busting through and ran after me. As I finally broke through the crowd, the bomber suddenly appeared before me. He had taken his first step onto the bus, and I closed in from behind. He looked anxiously from side to side for ISAF. He never saw the freight train coming.

Shoving people aside, I leveled out and tackled him from behind as he boarded the bus. I hit him hard, bringing him to the ground. Little did I know at the time that the sharp pain I felt in my leg when I landed on top of the bomber was my left leg fracturing. Suddenly I was face to face with him, and he was sandwiched between the pavement and me. He looked up at me, and his eyes were bigger than saucers. He had that look of shock and fear all meshed together.

Now what do I do? I am an old man attached to a young buck about to get either busted up or blown up. I only had a split second for him to realize that at that moment I was alone and unable to get to my gun without letting him go and giving him a chance to reach the detonator in his vest. His bomb had flown off to our side about fifteen feet from where we were pancaked on the asphalt. In the split second that I faced him, I remembered getting whipped in high school by an underclassman wrestler I outweighed by thirty pounds. That was a lot, considering I only weighed 128 pounds back in those days. He wrapped his legs around my head, and any time I moved an inch, he just squeezed till my pimples popped. I couldn't do a thing. It is amazing the things that come to mind when you are in a tight spot.

If I could just flip this bomber over on his belly and get him in a headlock, I hoped I could hammer down on him. So I grabbed him around the shoulders, flipped him like a flapjack as I slid my right arm around his neck, and placed him in a headlock before he could whistle Dixie.

I gripped his left wrist with his arm extended out, which prevented him from reaching into his vest to detonate the bomb. My machinegun was jammed between us, and I had his right arm locked out as I pressed him into the pavement. Suddenly I felt a thud as Jeff landed on the bomber's right side like a Navy pilot belly-flopping on a Liberty flat top carrier; it was like he dropped from the sky as he crashed down on us both. Jeff grabbed hold of his right side to prevent the bomber from reaching under his body to the detonator.

The bomber kicked and flopped in a mad frenzy to get out from under us. We fought just as hard, but to keep Shaheed from detonating the IED. The detonator was in his vest. The IED laid undisturbed several feet from us on the ground. Every time he moved a muscle, I would clamp down on his neck, squeezing it till he would stop.

I heard screaming in the distance and looked up in the direction of all the racket. There were dozens of Afghans who gathered about twenty-five feet from us and watched what we were doing. A few screamed at us. The others just stared at us, like chickens looking at a card trick, wondering what we doing. The longer they stood there, the more agitated they became. One of them began to stir up the crowd. He pointed at us in an attempt to get the crowd to attack us.

The crowd joined in with this jihadist agitator and began to move towards us. Police officers also came, upset by our fighting with a fellow countryman. Little did they know that if the bomber had detonated the bomb they would all be floating around in a dust cloud for the next few centuries.

Jeff and I locked eyes and realized we were goners. Just then, the Norwegian soldier we had ridden with and our interpreter appeared beside us. The soldier drew down on the crowd forcing them back and the interpreter began to shout that we were the good guys and the guy we stopped was a very bad man. The crowd held for a moment, and I yelled at the interpreter to pick up the bomb and bring it closer to us. Not one of my smarter moments. But I did not want someone to grab it and run off.

The interpreter carefully lifted it and placed it beside us. Together, Jeff and I fought violently to hold him down till the Norwegians showed up for the party. The sole Norwegian communications soldier continued to stand off the crowd with his machinegun while the interpreter continued to try to calm down the crowd. I have to hand it to the interpreter—he had grit.

A larger, more agitated crowd began to move towards us and surrounded us, ignoring the Norwegian. They shook their fists at us, yelling, "Your pants are on fire…your pants are on fire!" in Farsi. At least that is what it sounded like. But the look on their faces and the fact that they were spitting made me think I might have misunderstood them. It did not look good for the home team.

The Norwegian soldier still pointed his weapon at them but they looked right past him at us nailing their buddy. Jeff and I figured we were toast. Suddenly the wind kicked up, and it felt like we were in the middle of a tornado. I looked up and saw a helicopter hovering above our heads. Chris, who had been dutifully relaying orders to us from the command center, had reached his limit. He knew we were goners unless he broke protocol and acted fast. He grabbed the reins from ISAF command and ordered a Dutch Apache helicopter to drop down on top of us to hold back the crowd. I could feel the wind of the blades chopping above our heads. This held back the crowd, but we did not know how long it would continue to do so.

The danger escalated at a fast pace, and we had to do something. I told Jeff we had to whack this dude. If he broke our hold on him and detonated the bomb we were crispy at best, but more likely carbon, lodged in some Afghan's pajamas.

My machine gun dangled from a sling and was wedged between us. I could not get to my pistol in my thigh holster without letting go of his neck. My left hand held his arm back from reaching under and detonating the bomb. Heck, I had run out of hands to put the hurt on this guy. I looked at Jeff and grunted, "I can't get to my gun. Jeff, you've got to do it." He pulled out his pistol and pressed the barrel against Shaheed's head. Now, I had this screwball in a chokehold and that barrel was mighty close to my head. I held on tight to his neck and pulled my face away from the point of impact.

The crowd came alive when they saw Jeff's gun pointing at the bomber's head. They seesawed back and forth towards us while glancing up at the helicopter, not sure what the air boys could do to stop them. The crowd picked up rocks and bottles and heaved them at us. An Afghan cop ran towards us shouting something and Jeff pointed his gun at him, which made him stop. I looked at Jeff, and he slammed his pistol back in his holster as he looked in the direction of the crowd.

I am an old man and even the adrenaline was not hiding all my aches and pains of holding down this bull. The Norwegians were nowhere in sight, the crowds were moments from sending us to Jesus, and I was getting real tired of smelling this guy's neck. We couldn't shoot him or the natives would get jumpy. I knew what had to be done. I had to choke the life out of this hamburger before he got lucky.

I squeezed tighter, increasing the pressure on his neck. He turned beet red but kept on fighting. I kept up the pressure until I finally choked off Shaheed, cutting off his carotid artery, which caused him to collapse in the sewage we struggled in.

I nodded at Jeff, and we settled down, but did not let go of him. I thought I had killed him, only to have him come to minutes later. I felt him bumping off the asphalt and starting to flail his arms again.

He was determined to set off that detonator. Not one to give up, I choked him off again. He passed out like a possum.

This time I didn't ease up on my grip around his neck. Apparently, I am not really good at killing people, because after a while, he woke up a second time and resumed squirming under our weight. I gave his neck a good snap and cut off the flow of blood to his brain, not letting go. He was down for the count, but not dead. He remained in that state till the Norwegian forces arrived.

Only two soldiers showed up, parting the crowds like Moses did the Red Sea. They were a welcome sight. We had fought this guy for about twenty minutes. I wondered why the crowd opened up for only two soldiers, when suddenly an ISAF Humvee loaded with more soldiers closed in behind them. We slowly disengaged from the now passed-out Shaheed, passed our prey on to the soldiers, and helped them secure Shaheed in the back of their vehicle. He awoke to find himself in the custody of the Norwegians. Merry Christmas, you heathen jihadist. We removed the remote control detonator in his vest and cordoned-off the area around the bomb.

The IED was a pressure cooker and was fused and loaded with over three kilograms (6.6 pounds) of high explosives and projectiles. It only took ten ounces (less than one pound) of high explosives to bring down Pan Am 103 over Lockerbie, Scotland in 1988. I was one lucky cowboy.

I did indeed sustain a fractured leg in the altercation, though at the time I thought I had just jammed my leg up. Jeff and I were cut from head to toe from the asphalt. Within the hour, our wounds festered up due to the overflowing sewage that we had fought in. I am glad I got my shots before getting to the sandbox. It was a good thing, as we were unable to shower until the completion of the mission the following day. We smelled like old, rotting sewage. We both looked and felt like we had just run a marathon.

The Swedish bomb squad rolled up and secured the IED, detonating it in a containment trailer. Due to the IED's volatility, they weren't interested in transporting it.

We turned over Shaheed to the security agents of the Afghan National Directorate of Security (NDS). This was the procedure for any arrest in Kabul involving a terror suspect. Now, that may not have been a good thing for Shaheed as his terror cell killed five of their agents, but we had little choice. The Afghan government was not set up for dealing with all the logistics involved in handling these matters and assigned the NDS to pick up Shaheed for processing. Personally, I thought it was a grand idea. Who better to bring a little love into this forlorn, misguided soul's life? One year later, they turned Shaheed (a Pakistani) over to the Pakistani intelligence agency (sort of like our CIA), and I have not heard of him since.

THE AXE

We had the bomber and the bomb and probably saved some lives, but we still had a bomb-making factory and a terror cell to take out. Once again, Jeff and I are DEA dudes and taking out terror cells is not in our job description. However, we had the source, which made us a valuable commodity. The source, Ahmed, knew exactly where the compound was.

Normally, ISAF would just get the coordinates and go out and light up the compound, but they didn't have them. The GPS had failed when Ahmed tried to engage it at the compound.

We loaded up in the Ford Exploder and headed to the ISAF Camp Julian in east Kabul to plan the raid on the terrorist compound where Ashraf, the leader, was holed up. The command structure was not real keen on taking a couple of DEA agents on this detail, and we weren't happy about not going along. They were concerned about stepping on ISAF's toes and wanted to preserve the protocols of allowing ISAF to handle the matter themselves. If a couple of cowboys went along for the ride, they might once again fire up the natives. It seemed as if we were at an impasse until they realized that without our source, they would not find the terror cell. Reluctantly, they invited us to the party. Now we were cooking with Crisco.

ISAF completed the operational plan and left the camp en route to the compound with about sixty Norwegian and Canadian Special Forces in transport vehicles. Jeff and I boarded one of the vehicles along with Ahmed, our ticket to the fun. We were going to take the vehicles as far as we could and dismount. The plan required Jeff and me to escort Ahmed while he led us to the compound on foot. It was about midnight and pitch dark because of the lack of streetlights and indoor lights in the adobe compounds that we passed. This neighborhood was so primitive that the only light we might have seen would have been from candles or kerosene lamps. Chilestoon was easily three hundred years old.

We drove as far as we could into the narrowing maze of adobe homes, but could only drive to within a quarter mile of the compound before we had to dismount the vehicles and set out on foot. While the forces were forming up, the Norwegian commander leaned over to us and whispered in his Nordic-tinged accent, "This could be a night of dark horrors." It sounded like something out of an old Dracula movie. We lit out.

Jeff and I led the forces through the winding alleys, using the source to show us the way. We all felt a little spooked out as we furtively looked for any sign that our presence was detected. We all knew that the residents in Chilestoon weren't in our fan club. We did not want to wake them up and spoke quietly as we watched the doorways, windows, and the rooftops.

The narrow road that we walked upon was edged with high adobe walls on either side, almost like a funnel, and dark—very dark. In DEA we called these kinds of surroundings a "tunnel of death." The Dominican drug traffickers would build walled tunnels through a house to contain agents when they were running warrants. As the agents entered the house and proceeded down these tunnels, the Dominicans would ambush the agents, who would be trapped with no cover to fire from. We too would find ourselves trapped if things went south, trapped between the high adobe walls inside this tunnel of death. Jeff and I watched the intersecting alleyways and the tops of the walls as we walked, looking for any sign of an ambush. We continued at a slow, soft-footed pace while the ISAF followed us. An Apache helicopter flew above at a distance as back up as we approached the compound and lined up outside the door to make entry. The Norwegians hit the door first, followed by the Canadians.

Inside the compound, there were forty-seven people, thirteen adult men plus women, children, and one cow. (I can't help it, but I can't resist saying that I think the cow's name was "Moostafa.") ISAF arrested all thirteen men present, all of which were suspected members of the terror cell. Chris and Stan rushed over to the compound to assist in the site exploitation. When we saw each other we broke out in high fives and embraced, congratulating each other on the mission.

The compound was built with adobe and had a mud staircase, which twisted upwards to a second floor room. All of the women and children were secured in the second floor room, while a search was conducted of the compound. A stash of bomb-making components, Russian artillery rounds, pressure cookers, wiring, and shrapnel were strewn about one downstairs room. There were trip wires stretched across the rooftops of the compound to signal any attempt to penetrate from above by an opposing force.

I walked around the compound with a young Norwegian soldier

and searched for anything that might be considered "evidence." All of a sudden, I noticed an axe that leaned up against the wall. The siren call of the ancient-looking weapon pulled me towards it, and I picked it up. It had some symbols stamped into its blade, with a roughly hewn tree branch for a handle. I could easily picture old Ishmael chopping down a tree with it millennia ago. Hmmm.

Now, I believe in all the rules of evidence. Secure it, bag it, tag it. These are century-old standard operating procedures used by law enforcement in all first world countries. But I wasn't in a first world country. There is some very fine print located on the final page of the rules for evidence according to Sellers Law. Written there on the last page is the only exception to securing evidence. It is clearly written that souvenirs in third world countries are not to be categorized as evidence and are therefore exempt from the rules governing the securing of evidence. One cannot travel to the other side of the world, tackle a suicide bomber, and not get a souvenir. It was going in my suitcase.

At the end of the raid, all of the adult males were turned over to the Afghan security forces. We were going to let them sort it out. The bomb-making factory was in plain sight, and therefore anyone found in the home was likely fully aware of what was going on there. The degree of their involvement had to be ascertained. Mohammed Ashraf, the leader of this nest of killers, tried to blend in with the rest of the prisoners as he was escorted back to the transport vehicles. Our snitch pointed him out from among the prisoners, and we pulled him from the ranks, passing this on to the Afghan security team. During the course of his interrogation, Ashraf admitted to having provided the bomb used to kill the five Afghan security agents in December 2003.

A final note on Ahmed, our snitch. His body was found stuffed in the trunk of a vehicle several months later. The vehicle was parked alongside a desolate road near a village in the Hindu Kush. We never knew if it was related to our operation, as he had disappeared immediately after the raid on the compound never to be seen alive again.

CHAPTER NINE

BAD BART SPOILED AGAIN

HE DID WHAT?

It was a long drive back to the embassy. I knew we were going to pay a heavy penalty for disobeying a direct order. I was willing to take the hit. I walked with Jeff through the compound and bid him goodnight as I dragged myself to my hooch inside the embassy compound and crashed without showering.

I was woken up by a Marine at daybreak and was told to report to the deputy chief of mission (DCM). Still reeking of sewage, I walked to the embassy and took the elevator up, all the while contemplating his possible reaction to my adventure. Come to think of it, I didn't know why I had to face the executioner alone—where was Jeff, my co-conspirator? Beats me. I guess since I was the senior agent (or senior citizen), I was the one they were going to hold accountable. All I knew was it didn't look good, as I disobeyed a direct order and other such stuff.

I considered the worst-case scenario. Would he kick me out of the country? Yeah, he could and probably would. He had the authority to have me escorted to the airport and send my bags on a later flight home without so much as a "See you later!" I knew DEA was not one of his favorite agencies, so how much less would he appreciate a couple of DEA cowboys running and gunning? It would not be the first time that he had kicked someone out of the country, and for something a lot less worse than what I did. I really thought my goose was cooked.

The doors to the elevator slowly opened, and I stepped out into the hallway. I walked down the corridor, which housed all the leadership in the embassy. I had to walk through several large rooms to get to his office. I entered his assistant's office and was greeted by his secretary, though the term "greeted" is a little generous. She gave me a hard once over and glared down at my muddied up boots, then scrunched up her nose like she smelled something foul. She had a half-burnt cigarette with two-inches of ash that dangled from her lips as she looked down her nose just above her reading glasses and in her gravelly voice snapped at me to sit down in the adjoining office to wait for him. I sat there like a schoolboy who just got caught shooting spit wads. Heck, I was fifty-two years old and about to end my career on the high note of being kicked out of a place no one wanted to be in anyway. Oh well, I told myself. It was no great loss, and I could just retire and fade into the sunset.

I heard voices in the room I had just left and realized it was the secretary telling the DCM that I was waiting on him in his office. He walked in and looked like my old high school principal used to before he meted out my swats. He walked past me to his desk and sat down without even acknowledging my presence.

He looked down at the papers stacked on his desk, stared at something written there, slowly raised his head, and quietly looked at me.

"I'm not happy with this situation. I was woken up this morning by one of my aides (who, I might add, had probably brought him breakfast in bed) and was told that you had tackled a suicide bomber. I want an explanation, and I want it right now."

I told him the story, leaving out anything that might be too incriminating. He became visibly agitated and said, "I'm responsible for all Americans in Afghanistan, including you, and I have total operational control of all DEA operations…"

I interrupted him and said, "You had better take that up with Washington, sir. I'm just a grunt. Look, I only tried to save some lives out there. Yeah, I guess I broke a few rules, but a man's got to do what a man's got to do, sir."

This Bad Bart looked as if he was a stick of dynamite, all lit up and ready to blow, when he eased back as if to regain control of his anger and settled down.

He begrudgingly said, "What you did was heroic, but these kinds of things are not to happen on my watch. If you do anything out of the ordinary again, I will see to it that you get kicked out of the country. It's not over. I am going to take it up with the ambassador when he gets back in country." He dismissed me angrily and never acknowledged my existence again (not that he ever had) when we crossed paths in the embassy.

My boss, John, was determined to get to the ambassador before the DCM did. He made it a point to stake out the ambassador's office. Sure enough, John caught the ambassador and followed him into the office. John went over the entire episode for the ambassador in rapid fire. He did not want to be interrupted by the DCM before he unloaded. The ambassador was astonished and exclaimed that we were "heroes…and very brave men!" In a letter he wrote later to commend us for our actions, he added to these comments with these words: "This is just the thing we needed to counteract the growing sentiments that our forces are here only for our selfish interests, and not that of the Afghan people." Thankfully, through John's initiative, he put an end to the matter. If the ambassador endorsed our actions, then the DCM had to pipe down and leave it alone.

The ambassador is and has always been a first class representative of our government. Following his stint in Afghanistan, he was nominated for and served as the ambassador in Iraq. The DCM, the Bad Bart in my story, moved on to Beijing, China. I hope he enjoys his ox stomach soup. I have been to China—and that food ain't Chinese.

The command staff at ISAF wrote, "Prior to this incident, the people of Kabul believed that coalition forces were only interested in securing their own safety and were disillusioned about their (ISAF'S) presence." Coalition leaders praised this event as a turning point in the relations between the people of Kabul and members of the coalition.

Lt. Col. Chris Costa later wrote, "None of this would have happened had it not been for the DEA's willingness to partner with the military. As a postscript to this success, using this operation as a successful template, several other similar operations were later executed on the outskirts of Kabul and the Surobi Valley. Each of these source-driven operations was successful, but it was the DEA team that led the way by forging an unlikely partnership. Tim Sellers challenged me to get the right tactical force energized to support their force protection intelligence. As a consequence of these successes, ISAF senior leadership recognized our efforts, and we were credited for helping ISAF go on the offensive; heretofore, efforts were reactive. Press articles from Oslo to New Zealand picked up on an operational offensive shift in Kabul. None of the press reporting reflected DEA's courageous role in an unprecedented partnership in Kabul, Afghanistan."

It is doubtless that many American, Allied, and Afghan lives were saved because of the apprehension of these perpetrators of heinous acts against the Afghan people, which in turn uplifted and renewed the Afghan's support of the United States. It was deemed by ISAF a heroic success, encouraging Norway and other members of NATO to continue their support of American efforts in Afghanistan during this phase of the war.

Jeff slept like a baby through the entire goings on in Bad Bart's office and John's update with the ambassador. I started on the paper to document this deal and looked up at the clock on the wall. It was 9:30am. Hmm. No Jeff. I wondered if he was at the mess hall eating or just sleeping in. He was probably still suffering from jet lag. He had no idea of the reaming I received on our behalf. I knew he would want to know how close he came to being sent back to New York.

I got up and walked over to his hooch and knocked on his door. Jeff answered, rubbing the sleep from his eyes.

"Hey, Tim."

"Jeff, you're not going to believe…"

"Look, Tim, I have been in this stone age country for five days and only bagged one stupid Hig dude. I'm bored. Can we run up to Jalalabad today and whack some Taliban?"

I just sighed, looked at my watch, and replied, "Sure, why not? Get dressed. You can't go up there wearing those stupid Daffy Duck boxers. Oh, leave the teddy."

HOME

I flew into the good Ol' USA about a month or so later and returned to El Paso, resuming my normal humdrum duties. There was barely a stir in the division upon my arrival. I recalled seeing the one young agent, the law school graduate, who had commented that the streets were too tough for old agents and that they had no business working enforcement anymore. He had said that older agents lost their ability to react or perform tactically and would put other agent's lives in jeopardy. He never brought up the subject of Afghanistan to me, but it was the elephant in the room from then on.

Old? Yep. Tired? Some—I felt aches and pains in places I never knew I used before. Oh, maybe he was right.

Months passed and I was just rocking along when I got called into the Assistant Special Agent in Charge Janet Selzer's office. She asked me to sit down and immediately told me congratulations. I looked at her, a little confused. She said I had been awarded the Award for Valor, DEA's highest award for bravery. She passed me a real plain-looking, flat box and shook my hand. I opened the box and pulled out a nice plaque.

I was a little embarrassed. I tried to act a little "aw shucks" but inside I busted at the seams. Janet was real proud about that too. She said that Jeff had been awarded the Award for Valor as well. She was a cop's cop kind of boss and always looked out for us street agents. She served time in Peru and whacked a lot of Shining Path terrorists who attacked one of our forward operation bases. She and Mike Perez, another El Paso agent, flew around in a helicopter machine-gunning the bad guys who fired on their base. She and Mike deserved this award more than me. But oh well, I was gonna keep it.

Months later, I was called into Janet's office again and told that I was to report to Headquarters to attend the US Attorney General's 53rd Annual Awards Ceremony to be held at Constitution Hall on August 31, 2005. During this annual ceremony, the US Attorney General presents awards to members of the US Justice Department including US attorneys, DEA agents, FBI agents, and other US Justice members who performed exceptionally well. He was going to present two US Attorney General's Awards for Exceptional Heroism this year. Jeff and I were the recipients.

The most amazing thing about this trip was the presence of my son and three of his buddies from his unit about to deploy to Iraq. They were asked to stand up for recognition by the heads of all the agencies during the presentation. They are the real heroes.

CHAPTER TEN

RIDING INTO THE SUNSET

END OF THE TRAIL

The American cowboy of the Old West lived an independent life of solitude, with the freedom to ride the ranges without the restrictions of barbed wire fencing. He drove his cattle from fast moving waters, storms, and rogue cattle rustlers as he free ranged through the Western frontier. He was set apart from the drunken gunslingers, train robbers, and "Bad Barts" of the 1800s because he chose to live by the Code of the West. He lived and died wearing his white hat, protected the ranchers from the robber barons, and rescued damsels in distress. All he ever asked in return was to die with his boots on.

Did the independent spirit of free ranging and standing up for the oppressed pass with the cowboys of old? For the last century, this flame has been carried in the hearts and minds of American boys as they grew into manhood. Their minds were set on fire with dime novels that portrayed the lives of early frontiersmen. Radio and television shows like *The Lone Ranger*, *Roy Rogers*, and *Bonanza* served as windows into the past—a close-up lesson on the Code of the West.

I was one of these young boys who always wanted to wear a white hat and stand toe-to-toe with the bad guys in a battle against the forces of evil. Young boys have been this way throughout generations of Americans and will continue as long as there are memories of the last cowboys who roamed in the Old West. Today, the ranks of the police and military are filled with these boys who have grown into men who live out these dreams.

The Royal Canadian Mounties' Dudley Do-Right inspired us all to thump Snidely Whiplash and rescue Nell from the railroad tracks moments before the train came rolling down the track. I am sure that Dudley Do-Right exemplified good behavior and rightly embraced the regulations of the Royal Canadian Mounted Police to the letter. Though many cops and DEA agents of old may not talk about it much, they may have applied Dudley's life lessons and methods to their actions with a little twist: We Americanized it by adding a pinch of bending the rules, skipping the paper, pounding the bad guy into the dirt, and running to the sound of the gunfire. We are not unlike the cowboys of the Old West, who rode roughshod across the prairies, conquering the wild territory with little more than a bedroll and a six-shooter.

Old, worn-out, retired DEA agents will tell you that the best days of being a narcotics agent have passed. The restrictive nature of rules and regulations, political correctness, and video recording cell phones have taken out all the fun in the job. These cowboys are slowly being fenced in by technology, laws, regulations, and pencil-necked stupidvisors.

What does this really accomplish? For one thing, I guess it protects us from ourselves and our brash actions that on occasion may lead to a train wreck. It succeeds in slowing down the rocket ride of the fast-paced undercover agent as he barrels down the road, keeping up with the soulless traffickers of the drug world. It snips our wings and shapes our methods with the sharp edge of a cookie cutter to smooth our rough edges.

As a result of this, we lose the boldness of quick action, the ability to slam dirtballs at breakneck speeds, and the courage to do the right thing regardless of the consequences.

You don't have to wear a Stetson and a pair of Tony Lama snakeskin boots to be a cowboy Narc. You only need the mindset that is forged in the streets of life, fighting crime with an iron fist or sometimes a feather (a gentle touch). Over the years, you learn to discern as Solomon would and grow the courage of a lion when confronted with dark things. We aren't really as one would imagine. We aren't dashing and handsome leading men, but rather, we're old porch dogs, slumbering with one eye open, waiting, and watching—ready for that mangy cat or passing car to foolishly cross our path. At that moment, we spring into action and leap from our feigned rest to give chase, bringing down those who would dare challenge us. I recall an old Turkish proverb that reads: "There is a sleeping lion in the heart of the brave." We may all look like a pack of porch dogs, but deep down inside, we have the heart of a lion.

We are the cowboys of American law enforcement, a dying breed cut off from living our dreams in this not-so-brave new world. When society demands the fencing in of the freestyle police work of old, the new generations of cowboys have no choice but to step in line, or they will lose their job (or even worse, face legal consequences). Unfortunately, what these new restrictions can't accomplish, the aging process will—a last generation of gun-toting cowboys are slowed down naturally by their aging bodies, broken down by the wear of wrestling bad guys, bailing from patrol cars, and kicking in doors in the dead of night. Over the years, we watch as our hair turns gray or turns loose, our eyes turn hard (along with our hearing), the barbed wire pain of arthritis creeps in, and we have to learn to walk with a hitch in our get-along due to old, fractured bones. In the end, it is our own aging bodies that, like a traitor, serve to fence us in when the bureaucratic managers could not. Father Time has reared his unkind hand and touched us all.

The Last Cowboy is a testament to these old warriors. May they live out the rest of their lives in peace surrounded by their grandchildren and warm cookies to make up for the days they spent as rough men in order to protect the lambs.

CPSIA information can be obtained at www.ICGtesting.com
Printed in the USA
BVOW04s0821231214

380563BV00027B/273/P